ENTER
THIS
WAY

Published in the United Kingdom by
Collins & Brown
43 Great Ormond Street
London WC1N 3HZ

An imprint of Pavilion Books Company Ltd

Illustrations by Nick Hardcastle

ISBN 978-1-911163-57-2

A CIP catalogue for this book is available from the British Library.

10 9 8 7 6 5 4 3 2 1

Reproduction by Mission, Hong Kong
Printed by Toppan Leefung Printing Ltd, China

This book can be ordered direct from the publisher at www.pavilionbooks.com

AMAZING MAGIC TRICKS

TO CONFOUND AND ASTOUND

CHRIS
STONE

COLLINS & BROWN

INTROD

Magic tricks have amazed us for thousand of years. These days, illusions and advanced magic tricks are so convincing, so utterly compelling to watch, that they must be real, surely? As unbelievable as some tricks may seem — from the simple 'wobbly coin' trick to the most complex deck shuffle — what we are watching is not real, it is pure deception. Sleight of hand, tricks of the mind and a beautifully orchestrated system of bluffs with intriguing psychology and perfomance, convince our brains into thinking that all this magical majesty must be happening. Moreover — and this is the most magical part of all — we are all quite happy to be deceived, for the world of suspended disbelief is a beautiful world indeed.

The world's greatest and most-celebrated magicians, conjurors and illusionists can make us believe the unbelievable, and the impossible seem possible. But, of course, just like everybody else, these conjurors had to start somewhere: they too had to learn the simple (but effective) card tricks, the easy (but imaginative) coin tricks and the basic (but totally mindboggling) sleight of hand tricks before advancing to more innovative, radical and daring performances.

UCTION

Amazing Magic Tricks will get you started on your way. It is a book of simple tricks, to master, to perfect and then to perform. It should be your entertaining companion on your first journey into the world of illusion, distraction, trickery and magic. So, if you want all that and much more, then breathe deep, concentrate your mind, turn the page and read on.

IMPORTANT NOTES FOR THE MAGICIAN

[Before you begin astounding people here are a few do's and don'ts to be mindful of.]

1 DON'T OVERDO IT!
It is always a mistake to do too many tricks. Four or five knockout tricks should be quite enough for one session. Leave them wanting more.

2 NEVER DIVULGE YOUR SECRETS!
If someone asks you 'How do you do it?' just answer, 'Very well!' or 'It's magic!'

3 NEVER REPEAT A TRICK
Unless you can create the same effect by using a totally different method, never repeat! Forewarned is forearmed — if an audience knows what is about to happen there is more chance that they will discover how it happens.

4 PEOPLE WILL BE WATCHING YOUR HANDS

Make sure your hands are clean (at the very least!).

5 PRACTICE MAKES PERFECT

Practise, practise, practise until you know the trick backwards and you can perform it in your sleep. The more you practise, the slicker you will become. Practise in front of the mirror so you can see how the trick looks from the spectator's point of view.

6 KNOW WHAT YOU ARE GOING TO SAY BEFORE YOU SAY IT

Your patter has to be practised as much as your technique. There is nothing worse than a waffling magician. You could write yourself a script or record it on tape to help you develop a smooth flow.

7 DON'T TRY TO MAKE YOUR AUDIENCE LOOK FOOLISH

Some people get annoyed if they cannot work out a trick. Explain beforehand that your object is to entertain them. If they knew how you did your tricks, it would not be worth doing them in the first place, would it?

8 TRICKS DO SOMETIMES GO WRONG!

It happens to the best of us! Figure out what went wrong and keep practising so that you don't make the same mistake twice.

9 SMILE!

TRICKS OF THE TRADE

Before we go any further, let's take a minute to concentrate on the basic card skills any amateur magician should know to put on a good show. While the following overhand false shuffle and forcing (over the page) are technically tricks in themselves, they are used predominantly as a means to an end in the performance of several of the card and coin tricks that appear in this book. Brush up on these techniques first of all to hone your skills as a magician.

OVERHAND FALSE SHUFFLE

Almost everyone is familiar with the standard card shuffle (lifting sections of cards from the back of the deck and placing them at the front and middle of the deck). But this has the effect of mixing all the cards up: a disaster if, as a magician, you are trying to keep track of a particular card.

So, you must instead give the impression of a random shuffle, while in fact 'loading' the deck to suit your trick.

To practise this — you must practise this! — put the four Aces on the top of the deck, lift the bottom half of the deck upwards as normal (1, this is called 'undercutting'). Your left thumb now draws a card off the top of this half so that it lands on the top of the four Aces. At the same time slide it inwards so that it projects about 0.5cm (¼ in) over the edge (this is called the 'injog'). Shuffle off the rest of the cards unevenly so that the fact that it is sticking out is a bit less obvious (2).

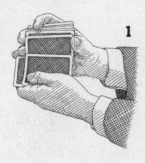

1

2

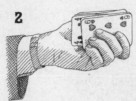

Draw off the top card into your left hand by dragging it there with your left thumb.

3

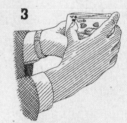

4

The card that was originally on top is now at the bottom.

5

6

7

'Undercut' the bottom half of the pack before placing the original bottom card on the top.

Your right hand now undercuts the deck again by pushing upwards on the underside of the injogged card (**3**), grasping all the cards below it and throwing them (still in one block) back on top (**4**).

If a trick requires you to shuffle the top card to the bottom, hold the complete deck in your right hand in the shuffling position (**5**). Draw off the top card only into your left hand by dragging it there with your left thumb (**6**). Now shuffle off the rest of the cards on top of this card. The card that was originally on top is now at the bottom.

To shuffle the bottom card to the top, just start a normal shuffle by undercutting the bottom half (**7**). Hang on to the original bottom card until last and deposit it on top as you complete the shuffle.

REVELATION!

DURING THE SECOND WORLD WAR, THE MAGICIAN JASPER MASKELYNE HID THE SUEZ CANAL AND ALEXANDRIA HARBOUR FROM THE GERMANS AND HELPED THE ALLIED FORCES WIN THE WAR IN AFRICA. IN THE BOOK *Top Secret*, MASKELYNE TELLS OF HIS WAR EXPERIENCES AND OF THE TIME WHEN HE PERFORMED AT THE EMPIRE THEATRE IN CAIRO, EGYPT, AS 'THE ROYAL COMMAND MAGICIAN'. FEW PEOPLE ACTUALLY REALIZED THAT THE PERFORMANCE WAS A FRONT FOR THE BRITISH INTELLIGENCE SERVICE.

FORCING

For certain effects it is necessary to force the volunteer to choose a specific card while apparently letting him have a completely free choice. There are several ways to achieve a force but the most relevant technique for the tricks that

follow is the cross-hand force. When you perform this, do not forget to emphasize the fairness of everything to your volunteer and the audience: you cannot see the cards, the volunteer shuffles repeatedly etc.

First, false shuffle the cards (see pages 10–12), then put them behind your back in your left hand. As soon as they are out of sight slip the card to be forced off the top and slide it over into the palm of your right hand, covering it with the back of your left hand. Turn around so that your back is now facing the volunteer.

Ask the volunteer to take the cards and give them a really good shuffle before returning them to your hand. Once he has done so, turn around again and slip the forced card to the top of the deck. Then invite the volunteer to take the card at the top of the deck. Easy when you know how!

VOODOO COIN VANISH AND PALM

Hold a coin in your left hand. Your other hand travels forward to meet it, the right thumb going under and the right fingers going over the coin. Make as if to grab the coin but as soon as it is hidden from view by your right fingers, let the coin drop secretly into your left palm. Complete the grabbing motion with your right hand, closing it into a fist. Do not move the left hand — merely grip the hidden coin with the second and third fingers. The right hand is now slowly opened — the coin has vanished!

Use your fingers to allow the coin to fall back into the palm of your left hand unseen by the audience.

COIN FOLD

Place a coin on a square piece of paper. First, fold the paper upwards crosswise from bottom to top, and then fold the left and right edges behind the coin. Finally you fold the top flap down behind. The coin now rests in the little packet, which, unknown to the volunteer, is open at the top.

While apparently creasing the folds of the paper packet more firmly, manoeuvre it until the open end is facing downwards. A slight squeeze on the sides causes the coin to slide out and onto your right fingers where it is palmed. The packet can now be burned or, at the appropriate time, opened up to show that the coin has gone.

Make the packet so that one edge is left open.

Holding the packet downwards, a slight squeeze will release the coin into your hand.

What does a magician say when they discover a jar of pasta sauce in the cupboard?

'HEY PESTO!'

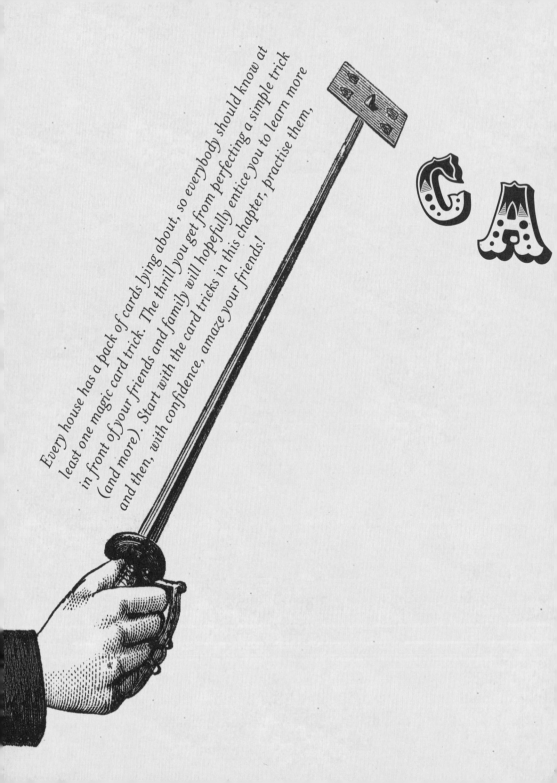

Every house has a pack of cards lying about, so everybody should know at least one magic card trick. The thrill you get from perfecting a simple trick in front of your friends and family will hopefully entice you to learn more (and more). Start with the card tricks in this chapter, practise them, and then, with confidence, amaze your friends!

CA

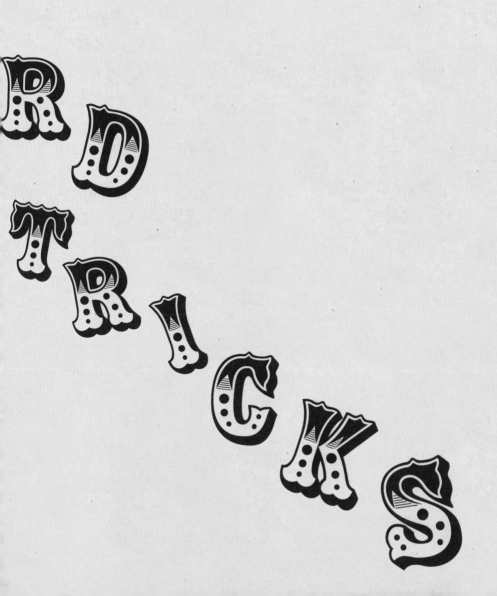

STICKY FINGERS

This unusual card trick will get you the attention you need to start your show. As if by magic a rosette of cards clings to your fingertips and remains suspended until the command is given for the cards to flutter to the floor.

WHAT YOU NEED
A pack of cards; clear sticky tape.

THE SETUP
Cut a piece of sticky tape and stick it to the back of a playing card to make a tab about 1.3cm (½in) long. When you do the trick, hold the tab between the knuckles of your second and third fingers to form an anchor card.

To maintain the impact of this flamboyant trick, make sure none of your careful preparation is spotted by your eagle-eyed audience.

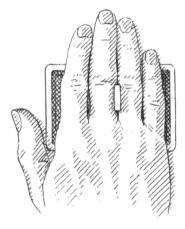

A tab of sticky tape will allow you to hold the card firmly between your fingers.

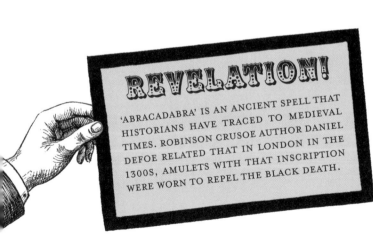

REVELATION!
'ABRACADABRA' IS AN ANCIENT SPELL THAT HISTORIANS HAVE TRACED TO MEDIEVAL TIMES. ROBINSON CRUSOE AUTHOR DANIEL DEFOE RELATED THAT IN LONDON IN THE 1300S, AMULETS WITH THAT INSCRIPTION WERE WORN TO REPEL THE BLACK DEATH.

THE PERFORMANCE

Secretly place the card and tab into position. Tuck the other cards under and around the tabbed card, which will anchor them in place.

Use about 12 cards in all until you have made a rosette of cards. Gripping the tab firmly between your fingers turn the rosette over to face your audience.

HEY PRESTO!

Hold the cards in the air and then command them to drop. Release your grip on the tab and the cards will flutter to the floor: and that's magic!

GOBSMACKER

After performing this trick your friends will think that you are totally brilliant, super skilful and a master magician. The name of a volunteer's chosen card is found written on a piece of paper that is concealed in your shoe.

WHAT YOU NEED

A deck of cards; a piece of paper bearing the appropriate message.

THE SETUP

To prepare, write these words on a piece of paper and sign it at the bottom: **'You are thinking of the Queen of Hearts'**. Fold the paper up and slip it in your right shoe. Place the Queen of Hearts on top of your deck of cards, get your patter ready in your mind and let's go...

THE PERFORMANCE

Get a volunteer, let's call him Simon. Give the cards an overhand false shuffle (see pages 10–12), retaining the Queen of Hearts on top. Then perform the cross-hand force (see page 13), which forces the Queen of Hearts.

Ask Simon to remember the card before he returns it and loses it in the deck when he shuffles them. Turn around to face him while he is still doing the final shuffle — now we lead him up the garden path a little.

'You shuffled the cards, chose one, returned it to the deck and shuffled again,' you say. 'Obviously, Simon, no one knows now where your card is, do they?'

He agrees that it would be most impossible! Take the deck back and start to look through them as if you are trying to find his chosen card. Then, with a look of triumph on your face, take out any card (not the Queen of Hearts) and, without showing it, place it face down under your right shoe.

'Your card is now under my right foot.'

Pick it up, turn it over and say, 'Tell me — yes or no — is that your card?'

'No.'

'Oh dear, can I try again?'

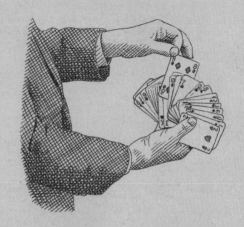

HEY PRESTO!

Take off your shoe, pick up the piece of paper and give it to Simon to read aloud. He will be absolutely gobsmacked.

THE SEE-THROUGH CARD

This classic of card magic is an absolute stunner, but choose your location and moment very carefully. Never attempt this trick unless the conditions are 100 per cent favourable – it is too good to be ruined by bad presentation – but if performed well, the volunteer's chosen card seemingly passes through solid glass!

WHAT YOU NEED
A suitable window with curtains that can be easily pushed aside; a duplicate of any card in your pack; double-sided sticky tape.

THE SETUP
Long before you perform this trick you must stick the duplicate card to the outside of the window so that it faces inwards; a small piece of double-sided sticky tape does the job nicely.

THE PERFORMANCE
Start with the five of Spades on top of the deck. False shuffle (see pages 10–12) a few times and then force the volunteer to choose the five of Spades by your favourite method. The cross-hand force (see page 13) works well here.

Once the volunteer (let's call him Jim) has remembered his card, returned it to the deck and given it a shuffle, give the deck to him to shuffle again. This is always a good policy when you do not have to keep track of a selected card. Just make sure he loses it in the deck. If you notice that he has shuffled the force card to the bottom ask him to give the cards another little shuffle.

'Let me have the deck now, Jim.'

Take it from him and walk over to the window. Your left hand pulls the curtain to one side while your right hand (which contains the cards) quickly puts the deck directly over the card that is outside the window. Your back helps to conceal what is actually happening, and as Jim has no idea what you are trying to do, you will find it easy to set yourself up in the correct position.

The cards, of course, must have their faces towards the room.

'Now Jim, I want you to take over from me. Come and hold the cards against the window for me please.'

You swap places and walk a few paces away, then turn to face him.

'What was the name of the card that you chose?'

'The five of Spades.'

'Please bring the cards to me now, Jim.' He does so.

'Look, Jim, you seem to have left one card behind stuck to the window. It is your card, the five of Spades! Would you fetch it for me please.'

TA DAH HA!

What did the fisherman say to the magician?

'PICK A COD ... ANY COD.'

HEY PRESTO!

In a daze Jim goes back to the window and tries to peel off his card. To his utter amazement he finds that, somehow, his chosen card has passed through the glass and is now on the outside of the window.

THE DREAM CARD

The volunteer finds your chosen card and yet has no idea how she does it. She handles the cards herself throughout.

WHAT YOU NEED
A deck of cards.

THE SETUP
No setup required.

THE PERFORMANCE
Give the deck of cards to the chosen volunteer (let's call her Suzy) and ask her to give them a thorough shuffle.

'Last night I dreamed I could see a playing card. Hold the deck up in front of me and pass the cards from one hand to the other, one at a time, so that I can see their faces. I want to find the card that I dreamed about. Just stop when I tell you.'

At this point you do not really have a card in your mind. Instead you must pay particular attention to the first two cards she shows you. These dictate which card you will pretend to be dreaming about. Use the value of the first card and the suit of the second card to determine your choice. For example, if the first card that she shows you is the nine of Clubs and the second the Queen of Hearts you must look out for the nine of Hearts – your 'Dream Card'. When it appears you call out 'Stop'. (If the first two cards that she shows you are of the same suit, just ask her to give the cards another shuffle.)

Reach out and take the nine of Hearts and place it face down on the table without showing its face. Because Suzy has been passing the cards individually from hand to hand, the order of the deck has now been reversed and the nine of Clubs and Queen of Hearts are the top and second card from the top respectively.

Ask Suzy to start dealing the cards one at a time onto the table, stopping whenever she feels like it. The two key cards are now at the bottom of this pile. Then ask her to deal this single pile into two piles, evenly, one card at a time. Notice on which pile the last card (nine of Clubs) goes. Point to that pile.

'This pile will represent the value of my Dream Card – and the other pile the suit. Please turn the top card of each pile face up.'

The first card that she turns over is the nine of Clubs, then the Queen of Hearts from the other pile.

'So you reckon my dream card is the nine of Hearts. Turn it over and see if you are right.

Place the nine of Hearts face down on the table without showing its face.

HEY PRESTO!

She turns over your dream card. It is the nine of Hearts. Because it is self-working the Dream Card trick works like a dream every time.

THE CIRCUS CARD

This is an old fairground con trick often used to fleece the unwary. When you attempt to find a volunteer's chosen card she is convinced that you have made a mistake. Convinced enough to bet all her money on it! You turn the table on her in a very funny way.

WHAT YOU NEED
A deck of cards.

THE SETUP
No setup required.

THE PERFORMANCE
Get your volunteer (let's call her Mary) to shuffle the cards. As you take them back, discreetly peek at the bottom card and remember it. This card will be the key to finding the card Mary is about to choose. We'll assume that it is the three of Spades, but it could be any card. Spread the cards out and get Mary to choose any one she likes.

Ask her to put the card back on the top of the deck and then cut the cards so that her chosen card is buried somewhere in the middle. This puts your key card, the three of Spades right

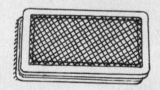

Cut the cards so that the volunteer's card will be directly under your key card.

on top of it! Get her to cut the deck two or three times. Just make sure that each time she merely cuts off the top half and then puts what was the bottom half on top of it. Don't let the two important cards become separated.

Tell Mary that you will be able to find her card without looking, just by touching the back of the cards. Hold the deck face down and slowly start to deal the cards face up one at a time onto the table, pretending that you are feeling each one. Keep doing this until you spot your key card. The next card you turn over will be Mary's chosen one (let's assume it's the four of Clubs). But don't let on. Place it face up like the others and continue turning cards over. After another five or six stop and say 'I bet you that the very next card I turn over will be the one that you chose.'

HEY PRESTO!
Mary will agree to the bet, knowing that her card has already passed through. As soon as she does agree put the card you are holding back on the pack and instead pick up the four of Clubs from the pile and turn it face down on the table.

MAGICAL STAGE NAMES

From the great magicians of literature like Merlin and Gandalf, to more contemporary comic conjurors like The Great Soprendo, Ali Bongo and Tommy Wonder, many magicians and wizards have unique names that capture the audience's attention as well as conveying a sense of mystery and enchantment in their act.

Once you have mastered your trick performance, and wish to perform your magic in front of an audience, you may want to choose a magician's stage name that suits or accentuates your personality.

A good place to start is to use one of the 25 magical names on the opposite page, followed by your middle name and your surname. Then add the phrase 'Magician Extraordinaire' afterwards for extra flair!

For example, 'Ladies and gentleman, my name is The Fantastical Robin Goodwin… magician extraordinaire!'

Now, try it with your name!

1. THE AWESOME …

2. THE BREATHTAKING …

3. THE MASTERFUL …

4. THE CAPTIVATING …

5. THE DAZZLING …

6. THE ELECTRIFYING …

7. THE ONE AND ONLY …

8. THE FANTASTICAL …

9. THE GREAT …

10. THE EXTRAORDINARY …

11. THE HAIR-RAISING …

12. THE INCREDIBLE …

13. THE GLORIOUS …

14. THE SENSATIONAL …

15. THE LUMINOUS …

16. THE MIRACULOUS …

17. THE MARVELLOUS …

18. THE UNBELIEVABLE …

19. THE MAGNIFICENT …

20. THE OUTSTANDING …

21. THE PHENOMENAL …

22. THE SPELLBINDING …

23. THE SPECTACULAR …

24. THE WONDERFUL …

25. THE ZANY …

A MATHEMATICAL CERTAINTY

For downright subtlety this classic takes some beating: you correctly name the cards that a volunteer hides in his pocket under what appear to be impossible conditions.

WHAT YOU NEED
A deck of cards.

THE SETUP
You must remember the names of the third and fourth cards from the bottom of the deck. If you make the third one the three of Hearts and the fourth one the four of Spades while you practise, you will find them easier to remember.

The key to this trick is remembering the names of the third and fourth cards from the bottom of the deck.

THE PERFORMANCE
Tell your volunteer (Paul) to cut the deck into two piles and then touch — not choose — one. You must get Paul to take the original bottom

half of the deck, seemingly of his own free will. If he touches it, get him to pick it up while you pick up the other half. If, however, he touches the original top half of the deck, pick it up yourself and invite him to take the other half.

Tell Paul you want him to duplicate everything that you do. You both count by dealing each of your set of cards onto the table, thus reversing their order. The noted two cards will now be the third and fourth cards from the top of his cut.

Announce the number of cards in your pack and ask how many he has. This is just misdirection. Whatever he announces, ask him to discard one. He will naturally discard the top one.

Take the top card of your pile and slip it into the centre. Wait while he copies you. Then take a card from the bottom and push it into the centre. Take another card from the top and put it in your left jacket pocket. Take another from the bottom and push it into the centre of the cards that you hold. Take one more card from the top and put it into your right jacket pocket. Replace your half of the deck on the table.

These actions have been deliberate red herrings. So long as Paul has been duplicating your actions, the card in his left hand coat pocket was originally the third from the bottom (three of Hearts) and the one in his right was originally fourth (four of Spades).

HEY PRESTO!

You bring the trick to its climax by first producing the card from your left hand pocket, naming it as you show it and then announce: 'It is a mathematical certainty that the card in your left hand pocket is the three of Hearts.' Then remove and name the card in your right hand pocket before correctly telling Paul that the card in his other pocket is the four of Spades.

THE REVERSED CARD

This super trick is very easy but at the same time very mystifying. A volunteer selects a card and then replaces it in the pack. The magician not only finds the chosen card, but reverses it in the pack as well. When performing this trick, take special care not to let your audience see the moves you are making with the cards.

WHAT YOU NEED
A deck of cards.

THE SETUP
To prepare the trick, turn over the bottom card of the pack so that the pack has two tops. Put the cards back in their case.

THE PERFORMANCE
Take the cards from their case and fan them behind your back. Be careful not to let anyone see the face-up card at the bottom of the pack. Ask a volunteer to select a card.

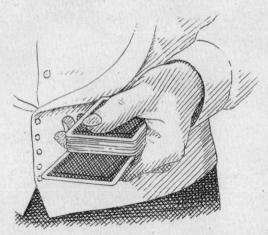

While the volunteer is looking at his card, square up the pack and turn it over so that the reversed card is at the top. Turn round to face your audience and hold the pack in your hand.

Take the volunteer's card and push it back into the pack. Hold the deck behind your back, and secretly turn the reversed top card over again. As you do this, explain that not only will you find the chosen card, but you will reverse it in the pack as well.

HEY PRESTO!

Fan out the cards face up on a table. The chosen card will be the only one in the pack which is face down, or face up if you hold the cards up to show your audience.

THE HOUDINI CARD

Harry Houdini was an American magician who lived from 1874–1926. He was known as an escape artist because no container, locks or chains could hold him – he always escaped! This trick is called the Houdini Card because the ten of Diamonds is firmly gripped in position between two other cards and only you know the secret of how it escapes.

WHAT YOU NEED

Two tens of Diamonds; one ten of Clubs; one ten of Spades; a clothes peg; a scarf.

THE SETUP

Hide one of the tens of Diamonds in your pocket. Now cut a sliver off each of the long edges of the ten of Clubs and ten of Spades. Cut a small rectangle in one short edge of the remaining ten of Diamonds.

Place the ten of Diamonds between the ten of Spades and the ten of Clubs with the cut edge at the bottom.

Before the performance prepare the cards as shown.

THE PERFORMANCE

Take the cards in your right hand and grip the lower left corner between your thumb and forefinger. Fan the cards out carefully to show the ten of Diamonds in the middle.

Close the cards and attach the clothes peg to the short edges of the cards. Ask a helper to hold the clothes peg. Cover the cards and the peg with a scarf. Hold the edge of the cards through the scarf with your right hand. Ask your helper to choose red or black. If he says black, pull away the scarf and at the same time secretly slide out the wide red card from between the two narrow black cards.

HEY PRESTO!

When your helper looks at the two black cards held by the peg, say, 'These are your black cards and my red card has flown into my pocket' (produce the card from its hiding place in your pocket).

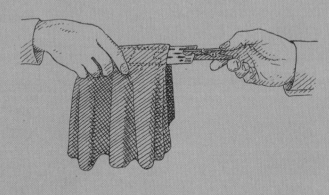

If your helper chooses red rather than black, for the last part of the performance you say instead, 'Your red card has disappeared from between the black cards and here it is in my pocket.'

CHOOSE A CARD

Here is a clever mind-reading trick that is sure to baffle your friends. With the help of some trick cards and a special 'scissor' move, you will be able to read the mind of your volunteer to reveal the card he was thinking about.

WHAT YOU NEED

Four playing cards; all-purpose glue; a top hat.

THE SETUP

Glue two cards, say the two of Diamonds and the eight of Clubs, back to back: this is called a 'double-facer'. Now glue two cards face to face: this is called a 'double-backer'.

Hold the cards between the thumb and fingers of your right hand, with the 'double-backer' on top and the eight of Clubs underneath. To practise the special 'scissor' move, turn your hand over to show the other side of the cards, and at the same time push your thumb to the left and your forefinger to the right in a scissor movement. This moves the double-facer across and allows the two of Diamonds to be shown. Reverse these moves when you turn your hand back again.

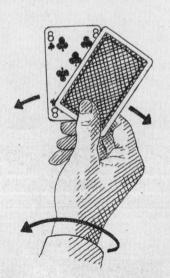 

THE PERFORMANCE

To present the trick, show the cards to your audience using the special scissor move and then drop them into a top hat. Ask someone to think of either card and tell him you will read his mind and reveal which card he was thinking of.

Reach inside the hat and take out the double-backer. At the same time have a sneaky look in the hat and note which side of the double-facer is showing. Hold up the double-backer. Say, 'It's not this one' and place the card in your pocket.

HEY PRESTO!

Now ask your helper which card he thought of. If he names the card that is face up in the hat, simply tilt the hat to show the card. If he names the other side, reach in to the hat and bring out the card with the side he named face up.

TA DAH HA!

Have you heard the joke about the magic tractor?

'IT TURNED INTO A FIELD.'

NO CHOICE

This clever card trick shows you how to make a member of your audience select the card that you want to be chosen. The secret lies in the way you set up the cards before you begin.

WHAT YOU NEED

A pack of cards; a large handkerchief.

THE SETUP

First take any card and place it face up on the bottom of the pack. Now put the card you want your volunteer to choose (for example the nine of Spades) face up under the first card.

Put the card you want your volunteer to choose face up at the bottom of the pack behind another card you have also placed face up at the bottom of the pack.

THE PERFORMANCE

Take the pack of cards and hold them face down in your left hand. Take care not to reveal the face up cards at the bottom of the pack.

Explain that you are going to ask a volunteer to cut the pack and then select the top card from the cards left in your hand. Tell your audience that you will cover the pack of cards with a handkerchief so that you will not be able to see your volunteer cutting the pack.

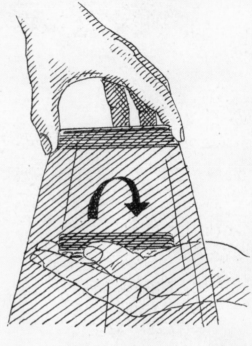

Now ask the volunteer to feel through the handkerchief and cut the pack. As he removes the cards and the handkerchief, secretly flip your pack over in your hand. The nine of Spades will now be on the top of the pack.

HEY PRESTO!

Offer the cards to the volunteer and ask him to select the top card. At the same time tell him that it will be the nine of Spades — which of course it is!

MAGIC SCISSORS

Here is a super card trick based on No Choice (see page 40). Your audience will be baffled when you produce cut-out representations of the cards they have chosen, only you know that the cards have been secretly set up beforehand so that your volunteers select the cards you want them to.

WHAT YOU NEED

A pack of cards; a handkerchief; scissors; a sheet of paper.

THE SETUP

Take the pack of cards and place any card face up on the bottom of the pack. Now place three cards, the eight of Hearts, eight of Spades and four of Diamonds, face up under the first card on the bottom of the pack. Memorize the order of the cards.

THE PERFORMANCE

Following the performance for No Choice, have three volunteers select the cards, but ask them not to tell you what they have selected.

Show a sheet of paper to your audience and fold it neatly in half four times. Explain that with the help of your magic scissors you will try to discover which three cards have been selected.

Ask the volunteer who chose the first card (the eight of Hearts) to concentrate on the card he selected. Carefully cut-out the first shape from your folded piece of paper. Ask your volunteer what the card is and open out the folded paper. It will have eight cut out Hearts.

Refold the paper and ask your second volunteer to concentrate on the card he selected. Now cut out the second shape, eight spades, from the paper. Ask your volunteer to name his card and open out the paper to reveal the eight of Spades.

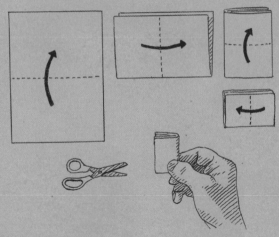

Now you come to your final volunteer. Refold the paper once again and ask your helper to concentrate on his card. Cut out the shape of four diamonds and ask for the name of the third card. When he says the four of Diamonds, hesitate and make a face.

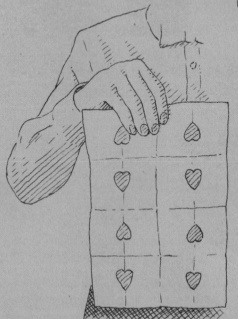

HEY PRESTO!

Everyone will think you have made a mistake and cut out another eight. You haven't of course, so smile and open the paper to reveal the four of Diamonds.

Fold the piece of paper as shown above and then cut out the required number of shapes for each card — eight hearts (as shown here), eight spades and then four diamonds.

EIGHT FAMOUS MAGICIANS OF THE 20TH & 21ST CENTURIES

There have been many amazing performers, illusionists and sorcerers over the past century. The magicians listed here are currently alive and kicking and, more importantly, wowing audiences all over the world.

1. CRISS ANGEL

Master American illusionist. Once walked across the water of a busy swimming pool as people swam underneath him. A neat trick, indeed.

2. DAVID COPPERFIELD

In 1983, Copperfield famously made the Statue of Liberty vanish and reappear, live on TV. He has also sawn himself in half and then, magically, put himself back together again.

3. DAVID BLAINE

Famous for his close-up street magic and for his grandiose stunts such as freezing, starving and burying himself ... live on TV.

4. PENN AND TELLER

Their most notorious trick, performed in front of an audience, is The Double Bullet Catch. Don't try this at home. An amazing double act.

5. LANCE BURTON

Do check out his infamous Roller Coaster trick, where he moved out of the way of a speeding roller coaster in Nevada, USA. The trick appears to have gone wrong with Burton himself exclaiming afterwards, visibly shaken, that it was a 'narrow escape'.

6. DYNAMO

Dynamo's 2011 'Magician Impossible' TV show pushed the limit of modern magic. Currently the UK's most popular magician, he is renowned internationally for his sleight of hand card (and mobile phone!) tricks as well as his mind-bending, gravity-defying unique adaptation of the levitation trick.

7. SIEGFRIED AND ROY

Daredevils Siegfried and Roy were known in the magic world as 'Masters of the Impossible'. As they performed and evolved their increasingly dangerous and over-the-top act, their show was often regarded as the most popular Las Vegas magic act on the strip.

8. DERREN BROWN

One of the most highly acclaimed British illusionists (and mentalists), currently performing to sell-out audiences. Known for his combination of 'magic, suggestion, psychology, misdirection and showmanship' as well as supermassive stunts such as performing Russian Roulette, predicting the National Lottery numbers live on TV and, in 2011, giving an ordinary man the confidence to land a passenger jet from 30,000ft (9,150m).

COIN

In these days of Chip and Pin and credit cards,
Next time you have a coin in your pocket,
to make money (if it's not your coin!)

TRICKS

coins are no longer stuffing up our wallets. Which is what makes these tricks so special. take it out, give it a polish and try out a vanishing coin trick — it's a good way and it's an even better way to impress your friends.

TEN MAGIC SONGS

Here is a selection of classic, and popular, songs to listen to as you practise your magic tricks. As you perform your act this playlist can be playing as you emerge onto the stage! Do you know any other magic songs?

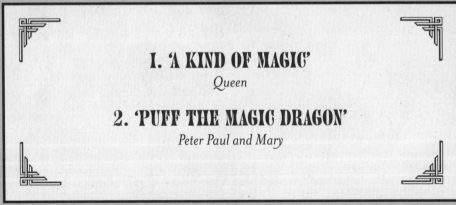

1. 'A KIND OF MAGIC'
Queen

2. 'PUFF THE MAGIC DRAGON'
Peter Paul and Mary

3. 'EVERY LITTLE THING SHE DOES IS MAGIC'
The Police

4. 'DO YOU BELIEVE IN MAGIC?'
The Lovin' Spoonful

5. 'COULD IT BE MAGIC?'
Barry Manilow

6. 'YOU MADE ME BELIEVE IN MAGIC'
Bay City Rollers

7. 'THE MAGIC NUMBER'
De La Soul

8. 'MAGICAL MYSTERY TOUR'
The Beatles

9. 'ABRACADABRA'
Steve Miller Band

10. 'IF IT'S MAGIC'
Stevie Wonder

THE BOLD COIN VANISH

Practising this trick will make the actions smooth and the effect extremely deceptive. A coin, apparently chosen from a handful of change, vanishes.

WHAT YOU NEED
A handful of coins of various denominations.

THE SETUP
No setup required.

THE PERFORMANCE
In order to perform this trick properly it is vital that the simple sequence of moves that are required exactly duplicate natural actions. So first, here is the natural sequence:

Take all the coins out of your right pocket and display them on your right palm. Reach across with your left hand (with its back towards your volunteer) and pick out one of the coins. Hold the coin between the fingers and thumb of the left hand and at the same time put all the other coins back in your pocket. Place the coin into your right hand, and close into a fist. Open your hand and show the coin. This sequence of moves must be practised until it becomes second nature to you. The success of the trick depends entirely on your ability to be natural.

To make a coin vanish, you must perform all these actions, only this time, when it comes to picking up the coin you don't! Yes, it is as simple as that. Remove the coins as before and display them on your palm. Reach over to take the coin with your left hand and, as soon as the back of your hand obscures the coin from sight, pretend to lift out a coin but let it slip out of your fingers again. Close your fingers over the imaginary coin and at the same time put all the coins back in your pocket again. Now pretend to pass the coin into your right hand and make a fist.

HEY PRESTO!

Now, at your leisure, make the imaginary coin vanish – both your hands are empty.

Sleight of hand will allow you to conceal the fact the coin has dropped back into your right hand.

REVELATION!

THE AUTHOR OF THE 14 MOST RECENT JAMES BOND THRILLERS WAS A MAGICIAN: JOHN GARDNER, RETAINED BY THE ESTATE OF IAN FLEMING, THE CREATOR OF THE BOND CHARACTER, WAS A PROFESSIONAL MAGICIAN BEFORE HE BECAME AN AUTHOR.

PENETRATION

You would be hard-pressed to find a better bar trick than this. A borrowed marked coin is made to pass magically into a sealed glass tumbler in full view.

WHAT YOU NEED

A glass tumbler; a drink coaster; a coin (the bigger the better); a small piece of paper about 10cm (4in) square; a pen; a small sticker.

THE SETUP

No setup required.

THE PERFORMANCE

Ask a volunteer to loan you a coin for the trick. Try to get the largest one he has. Have him mark the coin for future identification. As ink often smudges on coins have him mark the white sticker that you'll attach to the coin.

You are now going to do the coin fold (see page 15). After folding, the packet is given a little squeeze and the coin drops onto your right fingers, at which point you palm it. Take the packet away with your left hand and place it on the bar or table in full view. At the same time, with the coin still secretly concealed in your hand, pick up the coaster with your right thumb and index finger.

Turn your hand over and the coaster will automatically slide over to cover the palmed coin. Place the coaster over the mouth of the glass. In so doing it is easy to trap the coin between it and the lip of the glass. Let go. The coin will stay in place under the coaster, hidden from view, leaving your hands empty. Pick up the paper packet and place it on top of the coaster.

HEY PRESTO!

Show that your hands are empty and then give the packet a sharp tap with your finger. This will dislodge the trapped coin and it will fall into the bottom of the glass: it looks for all the world as if it has penetrated right through the coaster. Let the volunteer remove the coaster and the coin from the glass. He can see from his identification mark that it's definitely his coin. That's magic!

Tap the packet to dislodge the coin concealed beneath the coaster so that it falls into the glass.

REVELATION!

MATTHEW BUCHINGER, ONE OF THE PREMIER CUP AND BALL PERFORMERS OF THE 18TH CENTURY, WAS BORN WITHOUT ARMS OR LEGS AND WAS ONLY 74CM (29IN) TALL.

THE SNAPPY
COIN TRICK

Coin tricks are always fun to do and this is probably one of the fastest. You openly drop a coin into your sleeve and then magically pluck it through the cloth at your elbow.

WHAT YOU NEED
A small coin.

THE SETUP
You must wear a jacket. First you must learn and practise the snap vanish of a coin. This is really an optical illusion — very easy to do — but most deceptive.

Hold the coin between your right index finger and thumb, force the finger and thumb together with a snap, and the coin apparently vanishes.

What actually happens is that the bottom edge of the coin slides away across your thumb and the top edge drops and, as you grip it, it becomes hidden by the fleshy parts of your finger and thumb. You will soon get the hang of it. Once you feel confident that you can do the Snap Vanish, proceed as described.

THE PERFORMANCE
Sit with your right side turned towards the audience. Bend your left arm and rest your left elbow on the table. Hold the coin over the opening of your left sleeve and perform the snap vanish. It will look as if you have dropped the coin down your sleeve. Don't move your right hand.

HEY PRESTO!

Lift your left arm up from the table until the elbow is in line with your right finger and thumb. Pluck at your left elbow a few times and then magically 'produce' the coin again.

Perform the snap vanish holding the coin over the opening of your left sleeve.

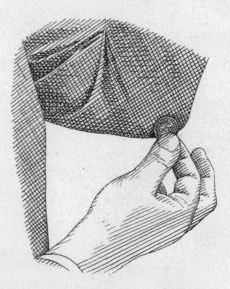

With the coin concealed in your right hand you can make your audience believe that the coin has passed through the material of your jacket.

MONEY TO BURN

Borrow the highest denomination banknote that you can persuade the volunteer to part with. Having sealed it in an envelope, you set fire to it, but then you resurrect it from the ashes and return it to your relieved volunteer.

WHAT YOU NEED
A borrowed banknote; a standard letter envelope; a box of matches; an ashtray; a deck of cards; a pen or pencil.

THE SETUP
Cut a 5cm (2in) slit in the envelope on the address side. If the envelope is shown flap side up, the slit should be hidden from view by the back pouch. Set up by

REVELATION!

THE MOST FAMOUS CHINESE MAGICIAN OF ALL TIME, CHUNG LING SOO, WAS REALLY AN AMERICAN NAMED WILLIAM E. ROBINSON. MORTALLY WOUNDED IN 1918 WHILE DOING THE BULLET CATCH TRICK ON STAGE IN LONDON. HE DIED THE FOLLOWING DAY, AND ONLY THEN DID THE WORLD DISCOVER THAT HE WAS NOT CHINESE.

putting the envelope and pencil in your inside jacket pocket. Put the matches and the deck of cards in your left jacket pocket. We will call the volunteer who lends you the money Neil.

THE PERFORMANCE

Talk to Neil: 'Lend me a banknote, Neil, and I'll show you a fantastic trick.'

Neil obliges and lends you a note. Take the pencil out of your pocket and hand it to him.

'In case you're fortunate enough to see your money again I would like you to sign your name across it.'

While he does this you remove the envelope from your pocket and place it (address side down) on the table.

'Did you know that money is virtually indestructible?
Let me show you …'

Take the signed banknote from Neil and fold it in half three times so that you end up with a little packet approximately 5cm (2in) square. Put the folded note on the table.

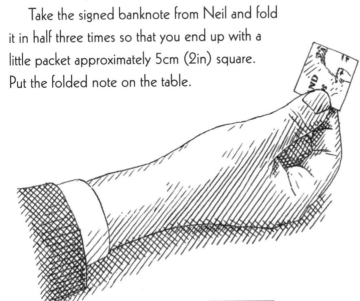

Hold the envelope in your left hand with your fingers covering the secret slit and your thumb on top. Pull back the flap with your right hand, pick up the note and push it into the envelope. The leading edge of the folded note goes through the secret slit on the outside of the envelope and you can hide it using your left fingers. Neil can still see part of his bill on the inside of the envelope.

Lift the flap up to your mouth by raising your left hand and lick the sticky flap. Lower your hand again so that Neil gets one last flash of his money, then fold the flap over and press it down to seal the envelope. Your right hand takes the envelope away and places it on the table. At the same time your left fingers hold on to his folded banknote and, without hesitation, you thrust your hand into your left jacket pocket. When your left hand is out of sight, push the folded note into the middle of the deck of cards.

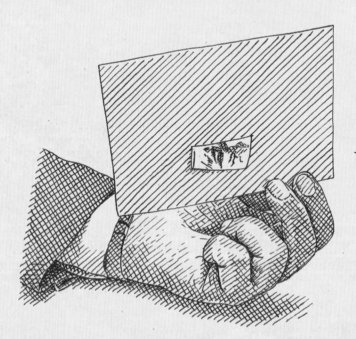

When you push the bank note into the prepared envelope it will pass through the secret slit so that you can remove it before setting fire to the envelope.

Leave it there and bring out the box of matches. Your two hands have moved in opposite directions simultaneously. The actions are very natural and because of this will not cause suspicion. Practise until you can synchronize the two actions smoothly.

'You will enjoy this, Neil. I'm going to set fire to your money. Please don't worry about it. I've done this trick before. Once!'

Pull the ashtray towards you. Strike a match and, then, holding the envelope by one corner, apply the flame to the diagonally opposite corner. Aim to destroy as much of the envelope as possible, especially the secret slit area. Be careful not to burn your fingers.

Now pretend this is all part of the plan. 'Neil, your money has withstood the heat and flames and will be unharmed. Let me show you.' Poke about in the ash for a couple of seconds before declaring with embarrassment. 'I'm very sorry, it seems to have gone wrong. Let me show you a card trick instead.'

HEY PRESTO!

Bring the deck out of your pocket and place it face down on the table. The banknote is inside of course. Tell Neil that you want him to cut the deck somewhere in the middle. He will automatically lift off all the cards above the folded note, bringing it into view in a surprising way.

'Ah, now I remember how to do this trick!'

Neil checks his note over for his identification mark. You can now remind him that it's his turn to buy the drinks.

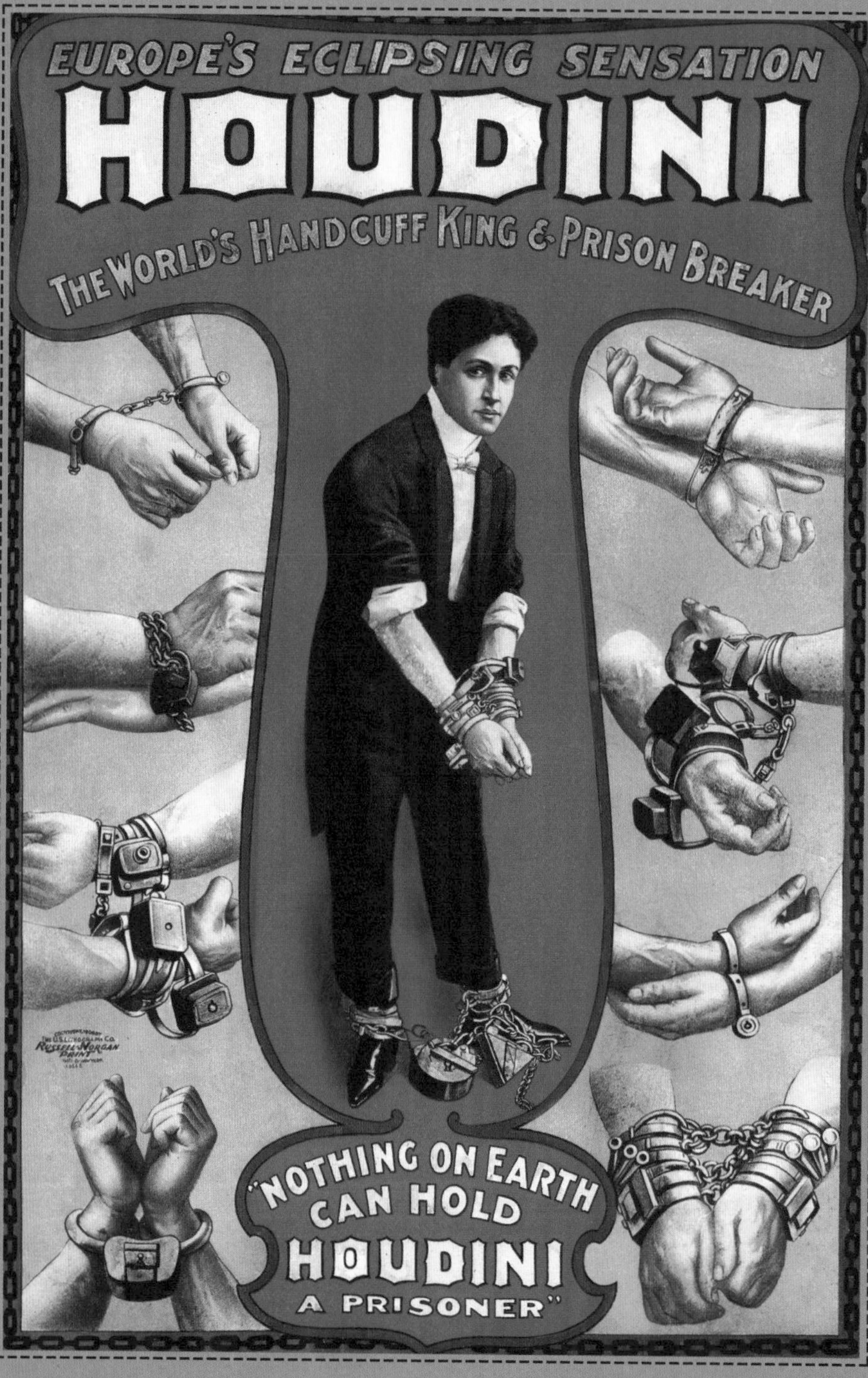
EUROPE'S ECLIPSING SENSATION
HOUDINI
THE WORLD'S HANDCUFF KING & PRISON BREAKER
"NOTHING ON EARTH
CAN HOLD
HOUDINI
A PRISONER"

THE AMAZING HARRY HOUDINI 1874–1926

Born Erik Weisz in Budapest, Hungary, Houdini began his magic career in 1891 under the name Harry 'Handcuff' Houdini. A self-proclaimed 'King of Cards', Houdini started performing traditional card tricks before going on to later focus his act on sensational escape feats for which he is most remembered. Like the popular American magician David Blaine in recent years, Houdini's stunts became more and more spectacular, sometimes leaving the magician himself close to mental and physical breakdown.

Many of his beloved, and best remembered, magic tricks are his cliffhanger escape stunts from chains and straitjackets while submerged underwater or while hung (and left swinging!) from the top of a tall building or crane. Many of his tricks would involve audience participation which, as many modern magicians would agree (due to the advent of TV and the potential of certain technology), make the more unbelievable stunts appear more realistic close up. One of Houdini's most notorious and remarkable death-defying feats was burying himself alive on three occasions. The first time he attempted this trick it almost cost him his life. He had to be pulled from the ground by his assistants after he lost consciousness after attempting to scramble away from the earth.

PIN TRICKS

Safety pins have many functions — from holding clothes up to keeping things from falling down. They are also great to use in magic! The tricks in this chapter will keep you entertained for hours, but always be careful when playing with any sharp objects. Make sure you are supervised at all times (the upside is you always have an audience!).

SPOOKY PINS

Two perfectly ordinary safety pins are firmly linked together. Or so it would seem! You hold one pin in each hand and pull in opposite directions. They become magically unlinked without opening.

WHAT YOU NEED

Two ordinary safety pins — try to find large ones as they will make the trick look more impressive.

THE SETUP

No setup required.

THE PERFORMANCE

Hold the pins precisely as shown, the pins should form a diamond shape between them in the centre. Note how the pins are joined through the middle but not interlocked. Once in the correct position, hold the pins firmly and pull your hands sharply in opposite directions.

When the pins are 'interlocked' properly together they should form a diamond shape between them.

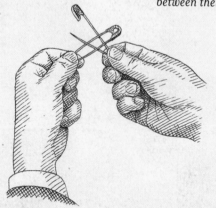

HEY PRESTO!

The pins will separate automatically. Practise until you can unlink them smoothly — you will soon get the knack.

HANKY PANKY

This safety pin trick looks impossible but is, in fact, entirely self-working. A safety pin is fastened to a handkerchief and you remove it without opening it.

WHAT YOU NEED
A large safety pin; a cotton handkerchief.

THE SETUP
No setup required.

THE PERFORMANCE
Spread the handkerchief out on the table. Fasten the safety pin onto the handkerchief near its edge. Turn the pin over to the left — three times. The handkerchief will of course roll over too. Firmly press down on the handkerchief with your left hand to hold it in place. Grip the protruding end of the pin between your right forefinger and thumb and pull down sharply.

HEY PRESTO!
The pin comes off cleanly and yet it is still closed. Return the undamaged handkerchief to the amazed volunteer.

A RIPPING YARN

A volunteer holds up her handkerchief before her. You fasten a safety pin in the hem at one end, give it a sharp pull, and the pin ends up at the other end, still fastened! Although a resounding ripping sound is heard the handkerchief remains undamaged.

WHAT YOU NEED
A large safety pin; a cotton handkerchief.

THE SETUP
No setup required.

THE PERFORMANCE
The volunteer should hold the handkerchief tautly. You should insert the safety pin at the point in the hem shown. Note that the solid (non-opening) bar of the pin should be to your left (below). **This is very important.**

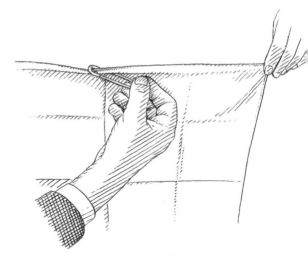

For this trick to work, the solid bar of the pin must be to your left.

HEY PRESTO!

Grip the end of the pin firmly and pull the pin sharply to the right for about 20cm (8in) and then push in. The pin will still be fastened but it is now at the other end of the handkerchief, and despite the sound of tearing the handkerchief will be intact.

I suggest that you try this on your own handkerchief until you get the hang of it — it shouldn't take too long. When you pull the pin to the right the bar disengages slightly from the clasp allowing the point of the pin to slide along the cloth without damaging it. You must push in at the end of your 'run' to make the pin penetrate the handkerchief again and so complete the illusion.

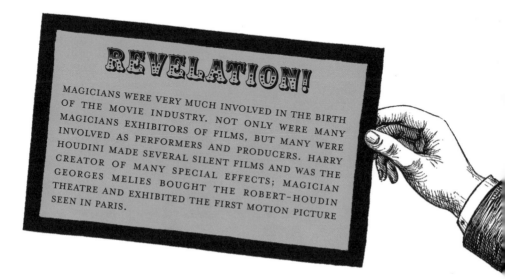

REVELATION!

MAGICIANS WERE VERY MUCH INVOLVED IN THE BIRTH OF THE MOVIE INDUSTRY. NOT ONLY WERE MANY MAGICIANS EXHIBITORS OF FILMS, BUT MANY WERE INVOLVED AS PERFORMERS AND PRODUCERS. HARRY HOUDINI MADE SEVERAL SILENT FILMS AND WAS THE CREATOR OF MANY SPECIAL EFFECTS; MAGICIAN GEORGES MELIES BOUGHT THE ROBERT-HOUDIN THEATRE AND EXHIBITED THE FIRST MOTION PICTURE SEEN IN PARIS.

MAGIC QUESTIONS & ANSWERS

Learning magic tricks is not just about fooling people for entertainment. It is also, as every magician would agree, a quest for truth, knowledge and expanding your mind.

So, how much do you know about magic? Below are five really cool terms, and skills, that every amateur conjurer should know if they are to convince their audiences they are a real magician. Test your skills with these five magic-related questions and then try them out on other magicians. Pass on the knowledge.

The answers are explained underneath. No peeking. How many did you get right?

1. **DURING A MAGIC TRICK, WHAT IS REFERRED TO AS 'A BURN'?**

2. **WHAT IS MEANT BY THE TERM 'SUCKER EFFECT'?**

3. **MENTALISM: WHAT IS IT?**

4. **WHAT DOES THE TERM 'EQUIVOQUE' MEAN?**

5. **DURING A TRICK, WHAT IS 'EXPOSURE'?**

---

1. It is when a member of the audience is forced to stare at the magician's hands without ever averting their gaze, no matter what misdirection is thrown at a subject.

2. A 'sucker effect' is a trick where the participant in a trick is led to believe they have worked out how the trick is done – only then to be proven wrong by the all-knowing magician.

3. Mentalism is a performing art in which the magician uses his five ordinary senses to create the illusion of a spooky sixth sense. Performers, such as the UK's Derren Brown, deceive or manipulate their audience into believing they are using supernatural abilities such as clairvoyance, telepathy and telekinesis.

4. Equivoque is the illusion of free choice when, in reality, the magician has already the predetermined the spectator's decision. The best example of this is the 'force' card trick technique, where the victim of the trick is led to believe they have chosen a card at random when they have, of course, taken the card the magician intended.

5. Sometimes a performer will, for the greater impact of the trick, intentionally reveal part (or all) of a trick for effect. This is called exposure. When a magician reveals part of the trick unintentionally this is called a mistake!

PIN IN A SPIN

This mini-miracle is a superb optical illusion. It will baffle even the most eagle-eyed audience. A matchstick repeatedly penetrates through the bar of a safety pin.

WHAT YOU NEED
A safety pin; a large matchstick.

THE SETUP
First cut the top off the matchstick leaving a length of about 6cm (2½ in). Then carefully push the pin through the centre of the matchstick. Take your time so that the matchstick does not split and the hole does not become too large. Twist the matchstick backward and forward until it revolves easily and freely on the bar.

THE PERFORMANCE
Hold the shield of the pin between your left index finger and thumb; make sure that the matchstick is impaled by the bar nearest you and rests under the bar furthest away from you.

HEY PRESTO!
To create the illusion that the matchstick penetrates the solid bar of the safety pin, just flick down sharply on the end nearest to you. The far end of the match will appear to penetrate the bar that it was resting under. It is now seen to be on the upper side of the bar.

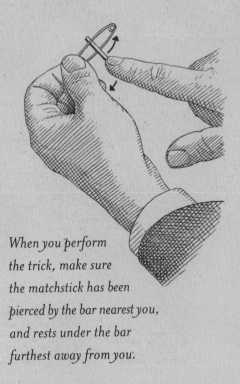

What actually happens is this: if you flick hard enough the matchstick will rebound and spin around in the opposite direction. It is really the end you flicked that has appeared to have penetrated the bar — the matchstick has turned full circle but too quickly to be followed by the naked eye.

When you perform the trick, make sure the matchstick has been pierced by the bar nearest you, and rests under the bar furthest away from you.

You will have to try this out in your own hands to appreciate the effect. It is very deceptive and can be repeated as often as you wish; you can flick the match upwards as well as downwards — it works either way.

TA DAH HA!

When I was a child my mother asked me what I wanted to be when I grew up. I said 'A Magician'.

SHE SAID, YOU CAN'T DO BOTH.

MAGIC
WORDS

*Here are eight magical phrases
that all amateur conjurors
should know. But, of course,
that should not stop you from
making up a few of your own!
Go on, have a go!*

1. HOCUS POCUS!

The provenance of this phrase is unclear. Many people believe it could be a corruption of the Latin phrase 'Hoc est corpus' (meaning 'This is my body'). Some believe it derives from Ochus Bochus, a demon in Norse folklore. Others equally believe it comes from the Welsh 'hovea pwca', a goblin's trick. Of course, it could have just been a made-up, nonsensical phrase that simply stuck around because it's fun to say!

2. ABRACADABRA!

This incantation has its first written recording in a 3rd-century AD book entitled 'Liber Medicinalis' by Quintus Serenus Sammonicus, a physician to the Roman emperor, Caracalla. It detailed that any person suffering from illness should wear an amulet with 'Abracadabra' inscribed in a triangle, as shown here, to ward off demons and aid healing.

```
A - B - R - A - C - A - D - A - B - R - A
A - B - R - A - C - A - D - A - B - R
A - B - R - A - C - A - D - A - B
A - B - R - A - C - A - D - A
A - B - R - A - C - A - D
A - B - R - A - C - A
A - B - R - A - C
A - B - R - A
A - B - R
A - B
A
```

3. TA-DAH!

This wonderful phrase has roots in, purportedly, mimicking the opening two notes of a trumpet fanfare, usually upon a grand entrance or announcement by a king or queen. The imitation of that sound phonetically is, simply, TA–DAH!

4. SIM SALA BIM!

Sim Sala Bim was first used, in magic circles at least, by Dante the Magician (1883–1955). Dante would use the phrase to mean 'a thousand thanks'. However, as the roots of the individual words come from Indian culture, it shows how some Western magicians would 'borrow' words from Eastern cultures to make their act sound more mysterious and magical.

5. OPEN SESAME!

Those of you lucky people who have read the fantastic adventures of 'Ali Baba and the Forty Thieves' will know that 'Open Sesame!' is the magical phrase that opens the cave where the treasure is hidden. Ali Baba is a character from Arabic medieval literature.

6. SHAZAM!

A fairly recent invention, Shazam! was first uttered in 1940 by Captain Marvel, a DC Comics character. In the comic book, Shazam was the name of a 3000-year-old wizard and when orphan Billy Batson says the phrase he is transformed into the amazing Captain Marvel. Shazam is actually an acronym of the names Solomon, Hercules, Atlas, Zeus, Achilles, Mercury.

7. HEY PRESTO!

Hey Presto! has been used by magicians and conjurors for centuries, recorded as far back as 1732. The origins of the word 'presto' are from the Italian meaning 'quickly' and 'presto' itself is a possible corruption of 'quick fingered' from the word 'prestidigitation', or 'sleight of hand'.

8. TIRRATARRATORRATARRATIRRATARRATUM!

Say it right first time (and out loud) and it'll be almost as amazing as any trick you attempt to accompany it. First recorded in the book 'Sammie and Suzie Littletail' in 1910, this magical tongue twister is a popular word to say onstage. Give it a whirl!

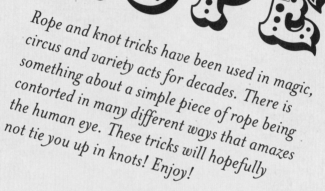

Rope and knot tricks have been used in magic, circus and variety acts for decades. There is something about a simple piece of rope being contorted in many different ways that amazes the human eye. These tricks will hopefully not tie you up in knots! Enjoy!

HANDCUFFED

Having trouble with noisy audience members? You may want to warn them that if they don't behave you have a magic trick that will tie them up in knots! You'll need to take two prisoners from your audience. Remember — only you will know how to set them free.

WHAT YOU NEED
Two pieces of cord or rope 1.5m (5ft) long.

THE SETUP
No setup required.

THE PERFORMANCE
To present this trick, you will need to tie each end of a rope to the wrists of the first victim. Do the same with the second victim, only this time, pass the rope over and under the first rope before tying it around the second wrist. Now tell your victims that they must try to free themselves without undoing any knots.

Give them a minute to try and figure it out.

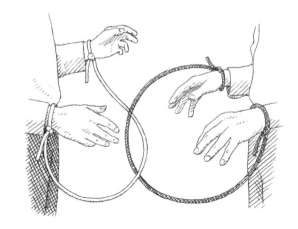

Tie the ends of two pieces of rope to the wrists of your volunteers so that they are joined together.

When they have given up trying, show them how it is done: take the centre of the rope from one victim and pass it through the rope tied around the wrist of the other victim.

Pull the rope to enlarge the loop as shown, and pass it over the hand. Now pull the loop down and tuck it through the wrist tie. Pull the rope back and away.

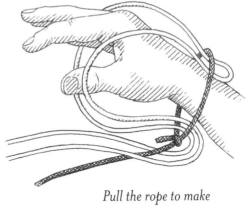

Pull the rope to make the loop bigger!

HEY PRESTO!

If you have done everything correctly the ropes will no longer be joined together and your victims will be free.

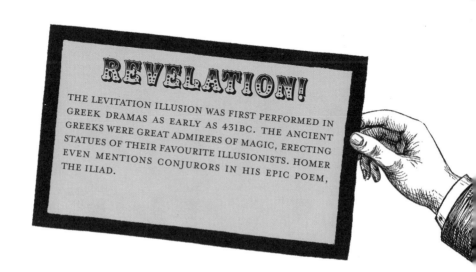

REVELATION!

THE LEVITATION ILLUSION WAS FIRST PERFORMED IN GREEK DRAMAS AS EARLY AS 431BC. THE ANCIENT GREEKS WERE GREAT ADMIRERS OF MAGIC, ERECTING STATUES OF THEIR FAVOURITE ILLUSIONISTS. HOMER EVEN MENTIONS CONJURORS IN HIS EPIC POEM, THE ILIAD.

BELIEVE IT OR KNOT

Watch the wooden beads fall to the floor leaving the cords mysteriously intact. The secret lies in the way the beads are threaded and knotted onto the cords. Practise this trick well before showing your friends.

WHAT YOU NEED

Five large beads; two pieces of cord 60cm (24in) long; a large handkerchief.

THE SETUP

Fold each length of cord in half. Push the centre of one piece through a bead and out the other side. Take the centre of the other piece of cord and push it through the loop sticking out of the bead. Pull the loops back inside the bead as shown in the illustration below (see inset). Thread the remaining four beads onto the cord, two beads either side of the centre bead.

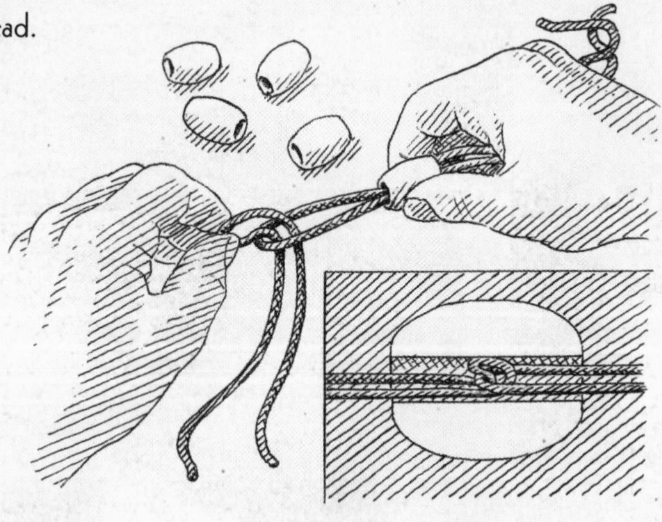

When you have made the loops push them back inside the bead as shown.

THE PERFORMANCE

To present the trick, show the bead necklace to your audience and ask for a volunteer to hold the ends of the cords.

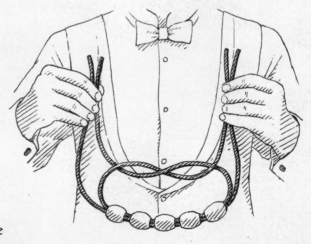

Say that the beads are securely threaded onto the cord, but to make sure you will take a cord from each of your volunteer's hands and tie them in a single knot. Make sure that after tying the knot the cord from the right hand is returning to the left hand and the cord from the left hand is returning to the right hand.

With your volunteer still holding the cords, cover the bead necklace with a handkerchief. Explain that you will attempt to remove the beads from the cord.

HEY PRESTO!

Reach under the handkerchief and release the wedged centre bead and all the others will follow. Take away the handkerchief and hold up the cords to show your audience that they are still intact.

CUT AND RESTORED ROPE

This is a classic trick that will take you no time at all to perfect. A long piece of rope is cut in half and then magically restored by tying some clever knots.

WHAT YOU NEED

A piece of rope or cord 1.4m (4¾ ft) long; a piece of rope or cord 10cm (4in) long; scissors; all-purpose glue.

THE SETUP

Glue the ends of the long piece of rope together to form a circle. Leave to dry. Form a loop in the rope on the opposite side of the join as shown. Insert a small piece of rope into the loop to look like a knot. Pull the rope to tighten the knot.

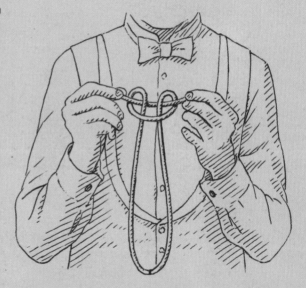

Make a dummy knot by forming a loop around a short piece of rope.

THE PERFORMANCE

To present the trick, show the rope to your audience. They will think it is a piece of rope tied with a knot. Cut through the glued join with the scissors and tie the ends together with a knot.

Hold the rope with the real knot in your right hand and the dummy knot in your left hand. Ask an audience member to call out left or right.

If 'left' is called out, say, 'I'll untie my knot.' If 'right' is called out say, 'I'll untie your knot.' Either way, untie the real knot. Take hold of the dummy knot, and trim the ends of the short piece of rope close to the loops.

HEY PRESTO!

Hold the rope in your hands with the trimmed dummy knot in the centre. Say a magic word and pull. The knot will fly off leaving the rope completely restored.

Hold the rope with the real knot in your right hand and the dummy knot in your left.

RING OFF

A ring is borrowed from a volunteer. You thread and knot it onto a piece of string. You magically remove the ring, even though both ends of the string are being held by the volunteer.

WHAT YOU NEED

A ring; a piece of string about 1m (3ft) long; a cotton handkerchief.

THE SETUP

No setup required.

THE PERFORMANCE

Having borrowed an expensive-looking ring, you thread and tie it onto the string. However, the special knot is not actually a knot at all! This false knot can be tied in front of the volunteer, provided you are very casual about it, and do not let him or her look too closely. Push the centre of the string through the ring and then feed the loose ends through the loop, tighten and work the knot down to the bottom. Hold an end of the string in each hand and display the ring, apparently securely tied to its centre. Hand the setup to the volunteer to hold in the same way.

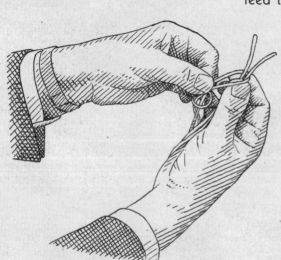

'While you are holding both ends of the string it is obviously impossible for me to remove your ring from the string – unless I saw it off.'

Drape the handkerchief over the ring and string and place both your hands beneath the handkerchief.

'Would you bring your hands a little closer together please.' The volunteer does this and so gives you a little 'slack' in the string to work with. To release the ring you merely have to work the centre of the string down and around the bottom of the ring.

Once you have worked the ring off, hold it against the string as if it was still tied on it. Conceal the part where the knot should be with your fingers, and take the handkerchief away with your other hand.

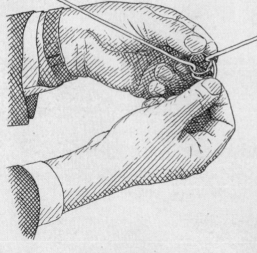

HEY PRESTO!

'I will count to three and your ring will come off the string.'

Pull downwards with your right hand, make a plucking action and return the ring, undamaged, to the astonished volunteer.

To free the ring from the string, work the centre of the string down and around the bottom of the ring.

TOP TEN
HARRY POTTER
MAGIC SPELLS

One of the most internationally famous fictional magicians ever, Harry Potter is responsible for popularizing magic for children and teenagers (and adults!) of the 21st century.

Not only that, of course, but J.K. Rowling's boy wizard has also encouraged children of all ages all over the world to pick up a book (a magic trick in itself!) and become passionate about reading fantastic stories again.

Also, these are just some fun phrases to shout out loud during your performance to add a bit of intrigue.

Try making up some phrases of your own!

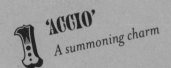 **1 'ACCIO'**
A summoning charm

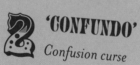 **2 'CONFUNDO'**
Confusion curse

 **3 'DELETRIUS'**
A vanishing spell

 4 'EXPELLIARMUS'
A disarming spell

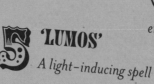 **6 'OBLIVIATE'**
A powerful memory-erasing charm

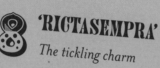 **5 'LUMOS'**
A light-inducing spell

 7 'REPARO'
Repairs objects

8 'RICTASEMPRA'
The tickling charm

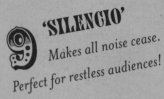 **9 'SILENCIO'**
Makes all noise cease. Perfect for restless audiences!

10 'WINGARDIUM LEVIOSA'
Lifts objects so that they float into the air

Magic tricks can take on many forms — from illusion to allusion, performance to distraction, coin tricks to rope tricks. The feats in this chapter are an assortment of the best tricks that you can do at home, both simple and fun. So, pick up your wand (or whatever you need!) and let's get started …

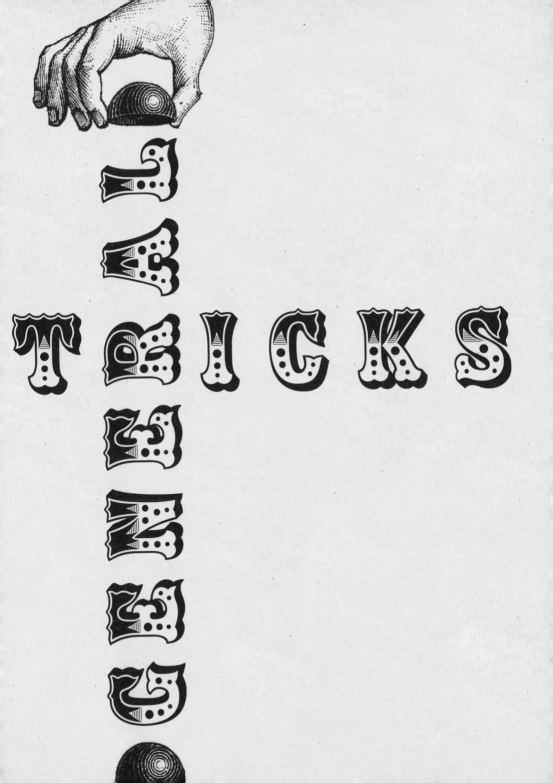

THE BOOK OF SPELLS

No magic show would be complete without a magic wand for weaving spells. Your audience will gasp in amazement as you conjure up your trusty wand out of a book of secret spells. Only you will know that the wand was up your sleeve all the time! Practise this trick in the mirror to get your moves smooth and the angles right.

WHAT YOU NEED
A magic wand; an elastic band; a small book.

THE SETUP
Slide the magic wand up your left sleeve and secure it to your wrist with an elastic band. Make sure the elastic band holds the wand firmly against your arm, but is loose enough for you to slip the wand out easily.

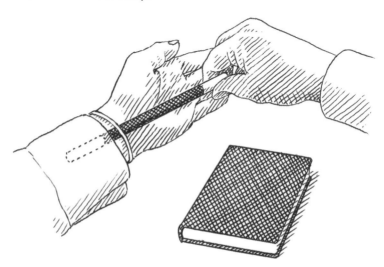

THE PERFORMANCE

Hold the book in your right hand and point to it with your left forefinger. Tell the audience that you need to look up an unusual magic spell in your book.

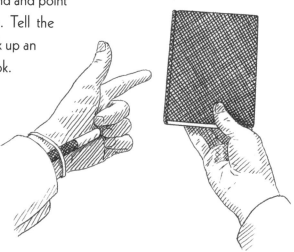

Flip open the book with your right hand and place it into your left hand. Look down at the book and tell your audience that it says you need a magic wand in order to perform your spell.

HEY PRESTO!

Reach inside the book with your right hand. Take hold of the wand and pull it out of your sleeve and into view. A big wand has been magically produced from a small book!

REVELATION!

THE WORD 'MAGIC' IS TAKEN FROM
THE PERSIAN WORD 'MAGUS',
WHICH DESIGNATED A PRIESTLY CLASS.

RISING RING AND WAND

Here we show you how to perform not just one but two mysterious tricks. Your audience will be amazed when you make a ring appear to move up and down your magic wand all by itself. And by the same method (a secret fine thread) you can make the wand rise too.

WHAT YOU NEED

A magic wand; some fine black thread; a small safety pin; a ring.

THE SETUP

Cut a length of thread about as long as your arm. Tie one end of the thread to the wand just above one end. Tie the other end of the thread to the safety pin. Pin the thread to your waist on the left side of your body. Make sure the safety pin is hidden under your belt or in a fold of clothing. Tuck the wand under your right arm.

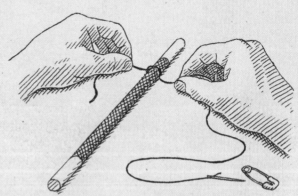

THE PERFORMANCE

Borrow a ring from a volunteer. Stand facing your audience so that they won't see the thread against your clothing. Take the wand in your left hand with the threaded end at the top and drop the ring over the wand. The ring will drop to the bottom of the wand taking the thread down with it.

HEY PRESTO!

Move the wand away from your body so that the thread is pulled taut, and the ring will rise up the wand in a mysterious manner.

You can make the wand rise too. To do this, push the threaded end of the wand into your fist. Hold the wand loosely at the top and move it away from your body. As you do this, the wand will rise up in your hand.

To make the wand rise, push the threaded end into your fist (A).

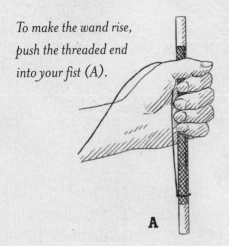

A

Hold the wand loosely at the top and move it away from your body. As you do so it will rise up (B).

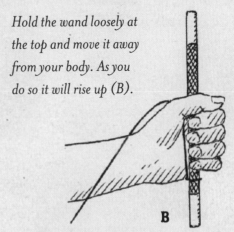

B

THE WONDER WIZARD

Make flat objects like coins, buttons and even postage stamps disappear into thin air with help of the Wonder Wizard. The secret to this trick is to use the same colour felt to cover the mouth of tumbler and for the mat. When the tumbler is placed over a flat object on the mat, the object will apparently disappear.

WHAT YOU NEED

An orange felt mat 46 x 30cm (18 x 12in); a plastic tumbler; a circle of orange felt cut to fit the mouth of the tumbler; thin yellow card; a coin; sticky tape; scissors; scraps of coloured card; all-purpose glue.

THE SETUP

Glue the circle of orange felt to the mouth of the tumbler. Now wrap the yellow card around the tumbler to form a cone. Hold the card in place with sticky tape.

3 IS THE MAGIC NUMBER

» *Think of a number*

» *Double it*

» *Add six*

» *Halve it*

» *Take away the number you started with*

* THE ANSWER IS ALWAYS 3 *

Trim the base of the cone so it stands up around the upside-down tumbler. Now decorate the cone to look like a wizard. Cut a beard, hat and arms from coloured card, glue to the cone, and then add face details and stars to give him that bit of extra magic.

THE PERFORMANCE

Set the tumbler face down next to the wizard and coin on the felt mat. Slip the wizard over the tumbler and stand both over the coin. Blow gently into the figure and say some magic words.

HEY PRESTO!

Lift off the wizard leaving the tumbler behind. The felt circle will hide the coin, which will appear to have vanished. To make the coin reappear, simply do the whole trick again in reverse order.

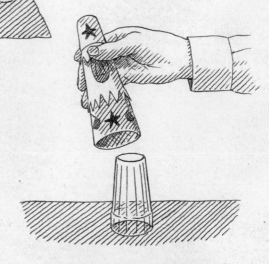

The felt circle covers the coin so it looks as if it has disappeared!

THE MONEY MAKER

Here is a useful magician's skill that will dumbfound your audience. It allows you to produce coins seemingly from thin air. Professional magicians usually take years to perfect this technique, but using the short cut shown here you can learn the trick in just a few minutes.

WHAT YOU NEED

Twelve large coins; clear sticky tape; a top hat; a small bowl.

THE SETUP

Fasten a tab of sticky tape to one of the coins. The tab should be long enough to be held between your fingers, without the tape showing on the other side of your hand.

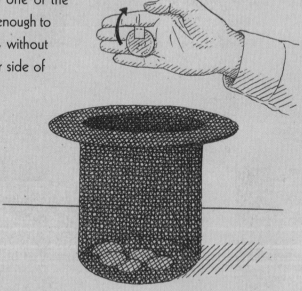

Hold the tab in position between the first and second fingers of your right hand. With the coin in the down position, and with the back of your hand facing the audience, the coin cannot be seen.

By putting your thumb under the coin and flipping it up, the coin looks as if it has been plucked from the air. When you have practised for a while, you will be ready to present your trick. Before you start, hide some coins in the top hat.

THE PERFORMANCE

To perform the trick, hold your hand over the hat with the coin in the down position. Flip up the coin, as if you have caught it in the air, remove your thumb and pretend to let the coin fall into the hat.

Pretend to catch a number of coins from the air and drop them one at a time into the hat.

HEY PRESTO!

Finish by tipping out the coins previously hidden in the hat into the bowl, to 'prove' you really did throw the coins into the hat.

 Tip! *To avoid suspicion remember to make the same number of* 'catches' *as there are coins in the hat.*

TA DAH HA!

What did the magician say when he produced a skewer of meat from his top hat?

'ABRA-KEBAB-RA.'

THE PENETRATING PEN MYSTERY

The penetrating pen mystery can be performed wherever you have a pen and a handkerchief. By making a special fold in the handkerchief you can make the pen appear to fall straight through the handkerchief as if it has magically penetrated the fabric.

WHAT YOU NEED
A pen or pencil; a large handkerchief.

THE SETUP
No setup required.

THE PERFORMANCE
Drape the handkerchief over your left hand. Allow more of the fabric to hang down on the audience's side.

Push your right forefinger into the handkerchief, between the thumb and forefinger of your left hand, to make a well.

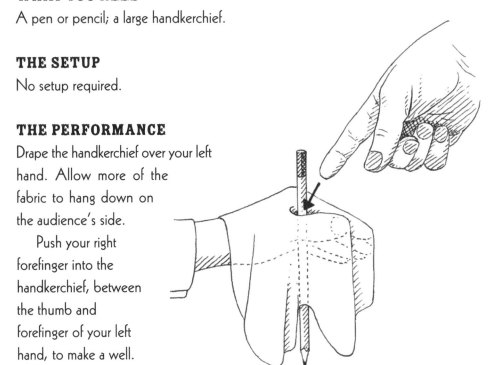

At the same time (most important!), secretly make a fold in the handkerchief with the second finger of your right hand.

Now pick up a pencil or pen and announce to your audience that you will make it drop straight through the handkerchief. Push the pencil into the secret fold.

HEY PRESTO!

Your audience will think it is going into the well, but the pencil will fall to the ground, penetrating the handkerchief.

TA DAH HA!

If Houdini were alive today, what would he be famous for?

HE'D BE THE OLDEST MAN ALIVE!

REVELATION!

FAMOUS MOVIE DIRECTOR ORSON WELLES HAD A LIFELONG INTEREST IN MAGIC. DURING THE SECOND WORLD WAR HE HAD HIS OWN MAGIC SHOW THAT HE PRESENTED FOR MEMBERS OF THE U.S. ARMED FORCES. HIS ASSISTANTS AT TIMES INCLUDED SUCH STARS AS RITA HAYWORTH AND MARLENE DIETRICH.

RING-IN RING-ON

All magicians know that the hand is sometimes quicker than the eye. This means that you can make your audience think they are seeing something that looks impossible but you know it is simply a trick of the hand. In this trick you can convince the audience that a solid plastic ring has threaded itself on to a length of rope, even though the two ends of the rope were in full view the whole time.

WHAT YOU NEED

A solid plastic ring or bracelet; a top hat; a length of rope or cord 75cm (30in) long; a length of rope or cord 25cm (10in) long.

THE SETUP

The set up of the table is important. You must keep one end of both ropes hidden behind the hat so the audience only sees one long length of rope. To do this, position the hat nearest to the audience, with the rope ends behind. Stand behind the table with the hat on your right-hand side.

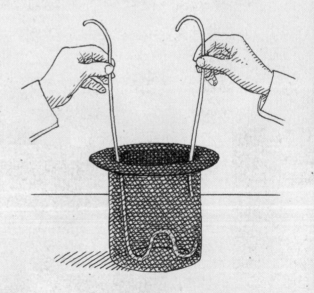

Secretly drop the right hand end of the long piece of rope into the hat.

THE PERFORMANCE

Pick up the pieces of rope, holding the ends of the short and long pieces in your right hand, so that the two pieces look like one length of rope. Lower the centre of the rope into the hat.

When your hands touch the edge of the hat, secretly drop the right hand end of the long piece of rope into the hat. Drape the left-hand end and the short piece of rope over the brim as shown.

Ask a member of the audience to hold the plastic ring and to make sure it is solid. Place the ring into the hat, secretly slipping it over the end of the long rope.

HEY PRESTO!

Mutter a magic word and pick up the two secret ends of the rope in your right hand and the other end in your left hand. Pull the rope from the hat to reveal that the ring has penetrated the rope.

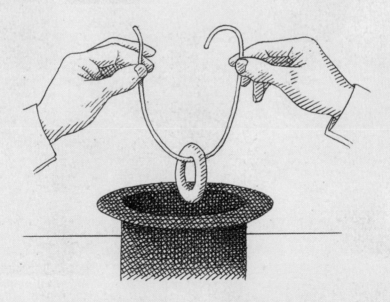

SLIPPERY SILK

The rope is knotted to the silk scarf, but the silk is also knotted to the rope. Your friends' eyes will pop out when you pull the scarf away from the rope with its knot still intact.

WHAT YOU NEED

A piece of soft rope 2m (6ft) long; a thin silk scarf 45cm (18in) square.

THE SETUP

No setup required.

THE PERFORMANCE

Pick up the rope and tug it to show that it is intact. Fold it in two. Make a loop in the rope as shown below, but tell your audience that you have formed a 'knot' in the middle of the rope. Take the silk scarf and pass it through the loop or 'knot'.

Tie a single loose knot with the scarf here!

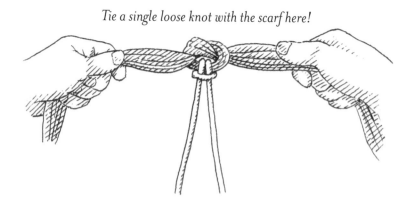

Pull the 'knot' tight and show your audience that the rope is knotted to the scarf. Tell your audience that you will now tie the scarf to the rope. Tie a single loose knot with the scarf as shown on the previous page.

Hold the rope about 30cm (12in) from either side of the 'knot' and tug the ends as if to show all is genuine. In actual fact this move upsets the knots and causes a large silk loop to form at the centre of the scarf. The scarf is now ready to be removed.

Put your left foot on one end of the rope and pull it taut with your left hand. Take hold of the scarf by the loop at the centre and slide it, with a sawing action, up and down the rope.

HEY PRESTO!

Pull the silk scarf sharply away from the rope and it will come free, still knotted!

REVELATION!

THE AMERICAN ILLUSIONIST DAVID COPPERFIELD IS KNOWN AS THE MOST SUCCESSFUL MAGICIAN IN THE WORLD DUE IN PART TO HIS CONTINUOUS SELL-OUT LAS VEGAS SHOWS AND SPECTACULAR STUNT SPECIALS ON TELEVISION.

TIGHTROPE BALL

You may need to spend some time practising this trick, but your hard work will be rewarded when you see the looks of amazement on your audience's faces. The ball looks as if it is balancing on the cord but, unknown to your audience, the ball is moving along a secret track you have made by tying a length of fine thread to the cord.

WHAT YOU NEED

A light plastic ball such as a ping-pong ball; thick cord 1m (3ft) long; a 60cm (24in) length of fine thread or nylon fishing line; a wine glass.

THE SETUP

Tie each end of the fine thread to the thick cord, as shown. Pick up the length of cords and place your thumbs between the cord and the thread. Pull the cord taut, so that the thread and cord form a track. You will need to practise doing this before you are ready to perform the trick.

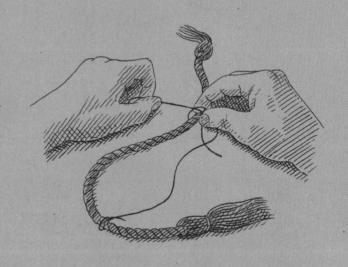

THE PERFORMANCE

Place the ball on the base of the wine glass. Pick up the length of cord and thread as you practised during the setup, and place it over the ball with the cord at the front and the thread at the back. Lower your hands until the cord and thread are level with the bottom of the ball.

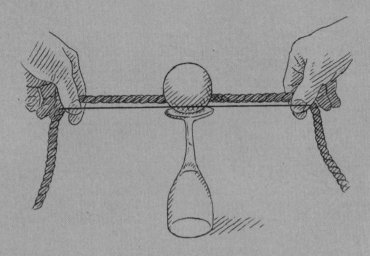

Invisible to the audience, the concealed thread allows you to apparently 'roll' the ball along the rope.

HEY PRESTO!

Pull the cord and thread taut and carefully pick the ball up onto the track. Move away from the wine glass. Gently tilt the cord to the right and then to the left. The ball will run up and down along the track.

THE BOX JUMPER

This is a dramatic trick often performed on stage and television by professional magicians. Your audience is shown what appears to be a perfectly empty cardboard box made up of two three-sided screens. They won't believe it when you clap your hands and your assistant pops out of the box.

WHAT YOU NEED

Two large cardboard cartons (e.g. washing machine boxes); a magic wand.

THE SETUP

Cut the top and bottom flaps, and one whole side from each carton to give two three-sided screens. Arrange the screens to form an enclosed box as shown with your assistant hidden inside. Notice the side marked X.

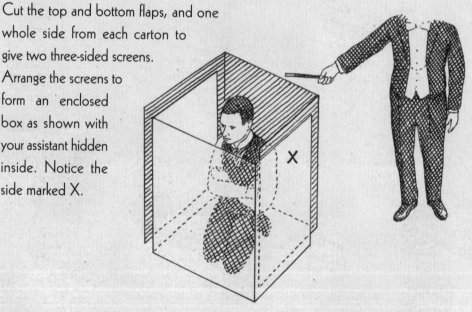

THE PERFORMANCE

Open side X slightly towards your audience. Pull out the rear carton and swing it round to show your audience. Replace the carton to your left by the side of the other carton so that it slightly overlaps the side marked X. While you do this, your assistant moves unseen into the (now) front carton.

Now pull out the carton your assistant had been hiding in, and swing it round to show your audience. Place the carton in position at the rear of the front carton.

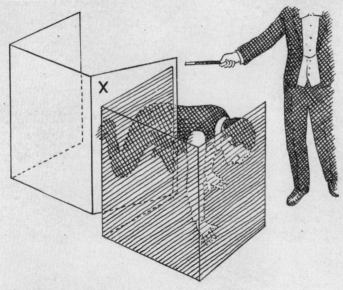

While hidden from the audience your assistant can crawl from one half of the box to the other before magically appearing.

HEY PRESTO!

Clap your hands, wave your magic wand and your assistant can stand up and pop out of the box.

THE FLOATING LADY

One of the most exciting tricks a magician can do is to levitate a human being. Now you can do this famous trick in your magic show too with the help of a friend who is good at keeping secrets. All you need is a large sheet and time to practise.

WHAT YOU NEED
A bed sheet or a long length of fabric; a magic wand.

THE SETUP
No setup required.

THE PERFORMANCE
Stand facing your audience and ask your friend to lie on her back on the floor in front of you.

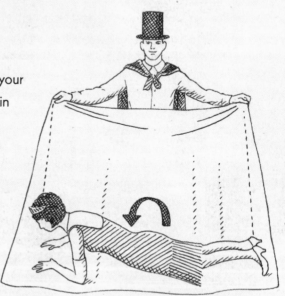

Cover your friend with the sheet. As you do this hold the sheet in front of your friend for just a couple of seconds so that she is hidden from view. As soon as she is out of sight she quickly turns face downwards.

Wave your magic wand and say a magic word. This is the cue for your friend to start to rise upwards. She does this by putting one leg out straight and raising herself up on her hands and the knee of her other leg.

HEY PRESTO!

Your friend should continue to rise up slowly until she is about 60cm (24in) above the floor. Say another magic word as the cue for her to start to lower herself slowly back to the floor.

Tip! *Make sure your friend remembers to turn herself back over before you pull off the sheet so you can take your bows ... without giving away the secret of your illusion.*

MAGIC PLACES

We all know there are many enchanting places in this beautiful world of ours. However, there are some places dotted around the globe that are still — after many years — more magical than others. And they sound it too!

If you fancy a holiday to a fantastical destination then why not head over to one (or all!) of these six bewitchingly named locations for a trip. Who knows, you might not want to come back!

1. SORCERER'S CASTLE, MONTREUX, SWITZERLAND

Most recently, and more officially, known as Chillon Castle. This beautiful, if spooky, castle has origins that date back to the 13th century. It is well known around the world as a once notorius hotspot for medieval sorcerers' tortures during the Dark Ages.

2. THE ENCHANTED FOREST, OBERURSEL, GERMANY

Located to the north west of Frankfurt, and second largest town in the strangely named county of Hochtaunuskreis, the forest is known for its enchanting beauty and massive diversity of flower and plant life. But don't go there after dark!

3. CASTLE HILL, HUDDERSFIELD, UK

This ancient monument sits all alone on a hilltop in the borough of Kirklees in Huddersfield. Many historians agree it is Yorkshire's earliest Iron Age hill fort and the most iconic landmark of the area. It is a place where local legend mixes with strange beauty.

4. NEUSCHWANSTEIN CASTLE, BAVARIA, GERMANY

This 19th-century ethereal Romanesque palace sits amazingly on top of a hill in Bavaria. Famed for its distinctive architecture, it has appeared in many magic-related movies and, most notably, was the inspiration for Disneyland's iconic Sleeping Beauty castle.

5. MOUNT COOK, NEW ZEALAND

At the foot of Mount Cook lies a body of water so intensely beautiful it has been referred to as the Magical Lagoon. The bright blue water mirrors the sky and the surrounding mountains so perfectly that visitors are unsure where the land ends and the sky begins — a truly bewitching place.

6. WIZARDS' TOWN, GENT, BELGIUM

Known affectionately to many as Wizards' Town, this strange region has awe-inspiring architecture and buildings that wouldn't look out of place in Harry Potter's magical world.

THE HAUNTED KEY

A large heavy key is laid across your palm. Merely by concentration you can make it come alive and turn itself over. They key is immediately handed out for examination. No trace of the method can be found – it must be haunted …

WHAT YOU NEED

The largest, heaviest key you can find.

THE SETUP

No setup required.

THE PERFORMANCE

This is a knack really. It will take a little practice but, just like riding a bicycle, it will suddenly come to you. Lay the key across your right palm. The exact position is very important. Notice that the flat part that is normally inserted into the lock is pointing back towards your wrist. The other end of the key must be free and not resting on your hand at all.

To perform this trick you need to make sure the flat part of the key is pointing towards your wrist, and the other end of the key is positioned over the side of your hand.

Look down at your hand, then very, very slightly dip your fingers towards the floor and, at the same time, will the key to turn over with your mind — this may sound crazy but it really helps!

HEY PRESTO!

Slowly and mysteriously the key turns itself over. At first you will probably find that the key rolls over very quickly, however, with a little practice and by varying the degree that you tip your fingers, you will be able to control the movement of the key completely so that it turns over very slowly, spookily and unexpectedly. Try it, you'll have fun!

TA DAH HA!

How do you get a magician to do 100 card tricks?

ASK HIM TO SHOW YOU ONE.

REVELATION!

DAVID COPPERFIELD WAS THE FIRST LIVING MAGICIAN TO HAVE A STAR ON THE FAMOUS WALK OF FAME IN HOLLYWOOD. THE ONLY OTHER MAGICIAN HONOURED WITH A STAR IS HARRY HOUDINI, WHO RECEIVED HIS STAR POSTHUMOUSLY.

SHORT AND SWEET

Somebody hands you a packet of sugar cubes from the bowl on the table. You place the packet on the back of your hand and tap it smartly with the other hand. The sugar cubes penetrate through your palm and plop into the coffee cup — leaving the crumpled wrapper still on top of your hand.

WHAT YOU NEED

Two packets of wrapped sugar cubes.

THE SETUP

When you find yourself in a café or restaurant that has wrapped sugar cubes on the table, secretly pocket one. Then excuse yourself and go to the lavatory. Once you are in private, carefully unwrap the sugar cubes. Put them in your pocket and then carefully reassemble the wrapper again. Moisten the adhesive flap and you will find that very likely it will stick down again and the package will resume its former shape even though it is now empty. Keep this empty parcel secretly cupped in your fingers as you return to the table. Be careful not to crush it.

THE PERFORMANCE

Palm the sugar cubes in your left hand with the empty package carefully palmed in your right fingers. As soon as the coffee has been served and before anyone can reach for the sugar you say, apparently on the spur of the moment: 'I've just had an idea for a trick — let's see if it works. Does anyone take sugar?'

When your friend hands you some sugar, take it with your right hand and place it about 10cm (4in) from the edge of the table and in line with your lap. With your right fingers draw the sugar package towards yourself with a sweeping action. Let the wrapped sugar cubes secretly fall into your lap and simultaneously bring the empty package into view, placing it on the back of your closed left fist. Practise this switch until you have got it down pat: it should look as if you have just picked up the sugar your friend has chosen and placed it on the back of your left fist.

HEY PRESTO!

Now position your left hand above the coffee cup, and synchronize these two actions: tap the wrapper smartly with your right fingers and at the same time open your left hand. The two sugar lumps then splash down into the coffee and the crumpled wrapper is left for examination.

The illusion of the sugar lumps penetrating your hand is perfect. Pocket the sugar cubes in your lap at your leisure. So there you have it: short and sweet.

As you squash the sugar wrapper release the cubes and allow them to fall into the coffee — hey presto!

PENCIL PUSHER

A pencil vanishes from your hands. This trick only takes three seconds to perform yet it is most effective given the right conditions.

WHAT YOU NEED
A pencil.

THE SETUP
No setup required.

THE PERFORMANCE
This trick is best performed to just one person. It is 99 per cent presentation. Although it is a small trick you must make a big show of it.
Have a pencil ready – borrowed if possible.
Stand with the volunteer on your left. Hold your left hand palm upwards in front of you. Hold the pencil in the writing position in your right hand. The following moves must be performed in a smooth, rhythmic sequence to the count of three.

Dad: Do you want to see the world's fastest magic trick?

SON: GO ON THEN.

Dad: Do you want to see it again?

'Watch closely, I will make this pencil pass through my hands.'
Bending your right arm at the elbow, swing your hand up in an arc until the pencil is level with the top of your right ear. Bring the hand down again, reversing the arc, and press the point of the pencil into your left hand. Count '1'. Repeat this whole process again and count '2' when you press the pencil into your hand.

HEY PRESTO!

On the third occasion, arc your arm up and place the pencil behind your right ear. Continue the motion down and press your hand as if the pencil was still there. Count '3'.

Display both your hands empty. The pencil has disappeared. Try this out – you will be amazed at how deceptive this is.

To make the pencil reappear reverse the whole procedure and retrieve the pencil from behind your ear after the count of '2'.

TA DAH HA!

How did the magician cut the sea in half?

'HE USED A SEA SAW.'

REVELATION!

ELIASER BAMBERG, THE 18TH-CENTURY DUTCH MAGICIAN, WAS KNOWN AS 'THE CRIPPLED DEVIL': HE HAD LOST ONE OF HIS LEGS IN AN EXPLOSION AND WORE A WOODEN LEG. ELIASER HOLLOWED OUT HIS WOODEN LEG AND USED IT AS A SECRET HIDING PLACE FOR HIS MAGIC PROPS.

CUP AND SPOON SORCERY

This mysterious trick is guaranteed to keep your audience guessing — so make sure you don't reveal your secret. The cup and silk scarf stay suspended on the spoon by means of a cleverly concealed magnet.

WHAT YOU NEED

A lightweight silk scarf; a small magnet; double-sided sticky tape; a plastic cup; a large metal spoon.

THE SETUP

Stick the magnet 3.5cm (1¹/₃in) from one corner of the silk scarf with double-sided tape.

THE PERFORMANCE

Hold the scarf in your right hand with your thumb hiding the magnet. Show the empty plastic cup to your audience with your left hand.

Place the cup over your right hand. Make sure that the corner of the scarf with the magnet attached is outside the cup.

Holding the rim of the cup with the fingers and thumb of your right hand, flip the cup over so that the scarf

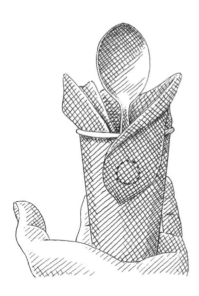

hangs over the mouth of the cup. Tuck the silk into the cup with your left hand.

Place the cup on your left palm, allowing the magnet to hang outside the cup. Make sure that the magnet faces you and not your audience.

HEY PRESTO!

Lower the handle of the spoon into the cup, remove your supporting hand and the cup and scarf will remain suspended on the spoon.

In this trick the magnet keeps the spoon standing in the cup when your hand is removed; make sure it is facing away from the audience.

REVELATION!

THE BULLET CATCH TRICK, WHEREBY A MARKED BULLET IS FIRED AT A PERFORMER WHO CATCHES IT BETWEEN HIS TEETH, IS THE MOST DANGEROUS ILLUSION IN MAGIC: IT HAS KILLED 12 MAGICIANS AND WOUNDED MANY MORE.

MIGHTIER THAN THE SWORD

A long strip of newspaper is shown on both sides. Boldly and deliberately the strip is cut in half and the two parts displayed separately. They are then placed together, given another snip and then a shake. Lo and behold, the two pieces have joined together into one long strip again.

WHAT YOU NEED

A newspaper; a pair of scissors; rubber cement (can be bought from high street stores and online); talcum powder.

THE SETUP

Cut a long strip of newspaper from the classified section. Avoid a strip with any distinctive photographs or other bold features. The strip should be at least 46cm (18in) long and 5cm (2in) wide. Paint a spread of rubber cement across the centre of the newspaper strip in a band about 5cm (2in) wide. Allow it to dry and then sprinkle talcum powder over the treated area. Blow off any surplus. When two surfaces that have been treated with rubber cement come into contact with one another they stick — this is the principle behind self-sealing envelopes. The talcum treatment prevents this from happening prematurely.

THE PERFORMANCE

Hold the strip of newspaper up by one end. Fold the strip in half so that the treated side goes to the outside. Cut the strip in half, through the centre loop. Display the two halves, one in each hand. Place the two halves together — this time with the treated sections on the inside.

Keeping the two halves aligned, just snip off a fraction of an inch from the ends. This cutting action has the effect of forcing the rubber cement from each section to weld together along the complete length of the cut edge. The talcum powder prevents a more widespread adhesion that would spoil the effect.

HEY PRESTO!
Let one end of the newspaper drop. The newspaper is restored!

Spread rubber cement across the centre of the newspaper strip in a band about 5cm (2in) wide.

COUNTER CHOICE

Follow the instructions for this trick carefully and you will be able to predict which colour counter your volunteer has chosen. Create an air of mystery and drama by telling your audience that you have the power to look into the future.

WHAT YOU NEED

Three counters — red, yellow and green; a small envelope and a piece of card to fit; some round stickers; three coloured pencils — red, yellow and green; a black felt-tip pen.

THE SETUP

Fasten a round sticker to the red counter and mark it with a cross. Draw three different coloured spots on the card and cross the green one. Now draw three different

coloured spots on the front of the envelope and cross the yellow one. Put the card and the three counters in the envelope.

THE PERFORMANCE

Hold the envelope with the spotted side facing down and tip the three counters on to a table. Put the envelope on one side. Explain that you will ask a volunteer to select a counter, but because you have the power to look into the future, you have predicted which colour counter he will choose.

HEY PRESTO!

Now ask a volunteer to select a counter. If he says red, pick up the counter and turn it over to show the cross on the sticker, proving your prediction was right. Also show that it is the only counter with a mark on the back.

If a green counter is chosen, take the card out of the envelope and show that the green spot has been crossed.

If your helper picks a yellow counter, turn over the envelope to show that the yellow spot is crossed. Whichever colour your helper chooses you are able to show that you predicted it. Of course, you cannot repeat this trick to the same audience!

REVELATION!

CHARLES DICKENS WAS AN
ENTHUSIASTIC AMATEUR MAGICIAN.

LAZY LINKING CHAINS

This is a spectacular trick that will go off with a bang! Magicians have always stunned audiences by making solid objects link up as if by magic. Here we show you how to make separate links appear to join together to make one long chain.

WHAT YOU NEED

A chain; a few separate chain links; two paper bags; all-purpose glue; a plastic tumbler; scissors.

THE SETUP

Cut one of the paper bags in half. Glue the bottom half of the bag to the inside of the second bag as shown, to make a secret inner bag. Place the chain in the bottom of the full-sized bag and the links in the plastic tumbler.

THE PERFORMANCE

Hold up the bag and drop the chain links from the tumbler into the inner bag. Drop the links in one at a time to show that they are really separate.

HEY PRESTO!

Close the inner bag and blow up the large outer bag. Twist the neck to keep the air in. Pop the large outer bag and pull out the long chain. The separate links will remain hidden in the inner bag.

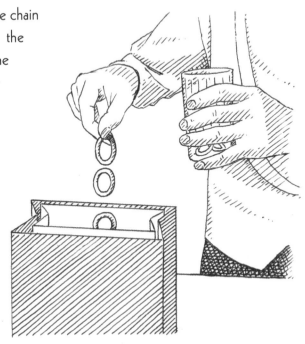

REVELATION!

THE WORLD'S FASTEST MAGICIAN IS ELDON D. WIGTON (DR ELDOONIE): HE PERFORMED 255 TRICKS IN TWO MINUTES ON 21 APRIL 1991.

THE DISAPPEARING DICE

Everything is not always as it appears in the mysterious world of magic. In this trick, a dice is isolated in the middle of a coaster and covered by cardboard tubes. Slowly the tubes are removed to reveal that the dice has — would you believe it! — vanished.

WHAT YOU NEED

A dice; a cardboard tube 4cm (1¹/₂in) high x 3cm (1¹/₄in) wide; a cardboard tube 7cm (2³/₄in) high x 4cm (1¹/₂in) wide; two drink coasters; double-sided sticky tape; single-sided sticky tape; wrapping paper; scissors.

THE SETUP

Cover the cardboard tubes with wrapping paper and seal the edges with sticky tape. Fix the dice to the centre of a coaster with double-sided tape.

THE PERFORMANCE

Place the coaster and the dice on the palm of your left hand. Cover the dice with the small tube followed by the larger tube. Place the second coaster upside-down on the top as shown.

Place your right hand on top of the coaster and turn the whole lot upside-down. As you do this, the small tube will drop down and hit the coaster. Your audience will

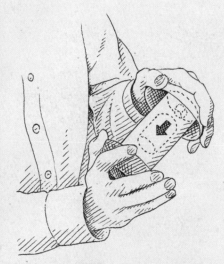

*When you turn the tubes
upside-down the smaller tube
will drop to the bottom.*

*Taking care not to reveal
the trick's secret, place the top
coaster under your arm.*

hear the sound, but they will think that the noise is being made by the dice falling through the tubes and hitting the coaster.

Lift off the top coaster with your left hand and, taking care not to let anyone see the attached dice, place it under your right arm.

HEY PRESTO!

Remove the large tube and then the small tube to show your audience that the dice has vanished from the coaster.

From close-up sleight of hand to enormous stage shows, these are just a handful of some of the world's greatest ever performed magic tricks by some of the world's most renowned illusionists. Don't try these at home!

1. DAVID COPPERFIELD'S DEATH SAW

Chained up, struggling and ultimately unable to break free in time, a huge swirling blade drops down on Copperfield sawing him in half. Though all is not what it seems, as the performer escapes in one piece!

2. THOMAS BLACKTHORNE SWALLOWS A JACKHAMMER

This wonderful piece of lunacy sees notorious sword-swallower Thomas Blackthorne swallow a jackhammer. This trick was performed live on a German TV show. And you thought swallowing a sword was crazy!

3. PENN AND TELLER'S DOUBLE BULLET CATCH

One of the most spectacular pieces of illusion carried out by the boisterous Penn and the silent Teller who fire bullets at each other, only to catch them simultaneously in their teeth.

4. RICHARD ROSS' LINKING RINGS

You really must watch the very elegant performance of the Polish magician Ross and his linking rings trick. The way he links, tangles and unlinks a series of rings together and breaks them apart is a lesson in first-class ring trickery!

5. HARRY BLACKSTONE JNR'S FLOATING LIGHT BULB

Watch as the bulb lights up and floats in mid-air, as the masterful performer waves rings around it, before handing it to an audience member to prove there is no invisible wire.

6. DAVID BLAINE'S STREET LEVITATION

David Blaine's incredibly popular 'street magic' TV shows in many ways brought it back to the street after decades of magic being predominantely seen at popular Las Vegas mega-shows. One of Blaine's most visually astounding tricks from his shows was his seemingly impossible trick of levitating his standing body completely off the ground.

MAGIC TRICKS

7. DERREN BROWN PREDICTS LOTTERY NUMBERS

The famous British mentalist predicts, correctly, each one of the National Lottery's numbers. People were divided as to how he actually achieved this ... with Brown's very own explanation of how he did it throwing up many questions. This trick was a great example of performance misdirection nonetheless for a master of misdirection and a magical piece of magical TV.

8. THE PENDRAGONS' 'METAMORPHOSIS'

The Pendragons are a married couple from America and this 'Metamorphosis' trick is consistently regarded as the fastest magic trick ever performed. Go check it out — you really do have to see it to believe it! But blink ... and you'll miss it!

ACKNOWLEDGEMENTS

Many thanks must go to the unbelievable Nick
Hardcastle for the magical illustrations, the breathtaking
Katie Hewett and Ian Allen for their all-seeing eyes,
the fabulous Gemma Wilson for laying the book out,
the sensational Claire Marshall for designing the book,
Malcolm Croft and Katie Cowan for their astounding ideas and
all the rest of the fantastic team at Pavilion Books.